The Saints of Qumrân

OTHER BOOKS BY RUDOLF KAYSER:

Die Zeit ohne Mythos (An Age without Myth)
Das junge deutsche Drama (The Young German Drama)
Stendhal oder das Leben eines Egotisten (Stendhal, or the Life of an Egotist)
Dichterköpfe (Literary Portraits)
Albert Einstein. A Biographical Portrait (written under pseudonym Anton Reiser)
Spinoza. Bildnis eines geistigen Helden (Spinoza. Portrait of a Spiritual Hero)
Kant
The Life and Time of Yehudah Halévi
Claude-Henri Graf Saint-Simon, Fürst der Armen (Claude-Henri Count Saint-Simon, Prince of Paupers)
Short Stories by Ludwig Achim von Arnim (Editor)
Verkündigung (Anthology of Lyric Poetry), (Editor)
Selected Works of J. G. Fichte and Wilhelm v. Humboldt (Editor)

RUDOLF KAYSER *was also a contributor to:*
The Universal Jewish Encyclopedia
The National Encyclopedia
Encyclopaedia Judaica
Lexikon des Judentums
The Stature of Thomas Mann, ed. Charles Neider
The Hebrew Impact on Western Civilization, ed. D. D. Runes

Rudolf Kayser around 1952

The Saints of Qumrân

Stories and Essays on Jewish Themes

Rudolf Kayser

Edited by Harry Zohn

Rutherford • Madison • Teaneck
Fairleigh Dickinson University Press
London: Associated University Presses

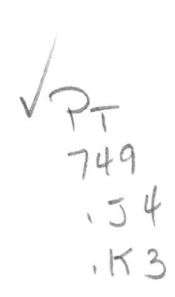

© 1977 by Eva A. Kayser

Associated University Presses, Inc.
Cranbury, New Jersey 08512

Associated University Presses
Magdalen House
136-148 Tooley Street
London SE1 2TT, England

Library of Congress Cataloging in Publication Data

Kayser, Rudolf, 1889-1964.
    The saints of Qumrân.

    Includes bibliographical references and index.
    CONTENTS: Zohn, H. Rudolf Kayser: an introduction.—Fiction: The saints of Qumrân. The death of Moses. [etc.]
    1. Jews in literature—Addresses, essays, lectures. 2. German literature—Jewish authors —History and criticism—Addresses, essays, lectures. 3. Moses—Fiction. 4. Spinoza, Benedictus de, 1632-1677. I. Zohn, Harry. II. Title.
PT749.J4K3 1977   838'.9'1208   76-20273
ISBN 0-8386-2024-8

PRINTED IN THE UNITED STATES OF AMERICA

The editor wishes to express his appreciation to Eva Kayser, without whose expertise and collaboration this book could not have come into being.

Contents

Acknowledgments 9
Rudolf Kayser: An Introduction by Harry Zohn 11

PART I Fiction

The Saints of Qumrân: A Story 23
The Death of Moses: A Legend 59
Here Am I!: A Story 70
David Plays Before Saul: A Poem 85

PART II Literary Essays

Lessing and Judaism 89
Bettina von Arnim and the Jews 94
Telling the News: A Chapter of Thomas Mann's Novel *Joseph the Provider* 107
The Nature and the Work of Martin Buber 114
In Memory of Franz Kafka (1946) 120
Jakob Wassermann 126
Moritz Heimann, 1868-1925 136
In Memoriam Albert Einstein 141

PART III Religion and Philosophy

Thoughts on Religion 149
Amor Dei: An Approach to Spinoza's Philosophy of Religion 161
Intuition and Knowledge: On the Henri Bergson Centennial, October 18, 1959 175
Aspects of the Jewish Question 180
Jewish Thoughts 186

Acknowledgments

The Saints of Qumrân was first published (in German) together with *Here Am I!* (in German) by the Hegereiter-Verlag, Rothenburg ob der Tauber, 1964.

Here Am I! appeared first in the Passover issue of *The Jewish Advocate*, Boston, on April 15, 1954.

The Death of Moses was published originally (in German) in the series *Der Jüngste Tag* of the Kurt Wolff Verlag, Munich, 1921.

"Bettina Von Arnim and the Jews" first appeared in *Historia Judaica* 20 (Editor Guido Kisch) (April 1958):47–60.

"Moritz Heimann" first appeared (in German) in *Israel-Forum* 9, no. 12 (December 1967).

"In Memory of Franz Kafka" first appeared (in German) in *Deutsche Blätter*, vol. 34, Santiago de Chile, 1946.

"Jakob Wassermann" first appeared in *The Jewish Forum* 9, no. 4 (June 1936).

"Telling the News" first appeared in the Thomas Mann issue of *The Germanic Review* 25, no. 4 (December 1950):285–89.

"Amor Dei" appeared first in *Horizons of a Philosopher. Essays in Honor of David Baumgardt*. Leiden: E. J. Brill, 1963.

"Intuition and Knowledge. On the Henri Bergson Centennial" first appeared (in German) in *Aufbau*, New York, October 23, 1959.

"The Nature and the Work of Martin Buber" first appeared in *Aufbau* 24, no. 6 (February 7, 1958).

"In Memoriam Albert Einstein" first appeared (in German) in *Helle Zeit—Dunkle Zeit. In Memoriam Albert Einstein*. Editor Carl Seelig. Zürich: Europa Verlag, 1956.

"Aspects of the Jewish Question" first appeared in *The Jewish Advocate*, Boston, August 18, 1960.

The permission of the above editors and publishers to reprint these materials is herewith gratefully acknowledged.

The photograph of Rudolf Kayser and Martin Buber and the frontispiece are reproduced with the permission of Ralph Norman, Brandeis University Photographer.

The photograph of Rudolf Kayser and Albert Einstein was taken by Eva Kayser.

Rudolf Kayser
An Introduction

Rudolf Kayser has been called "the last humanist" and also the "gentleman" and the "gentle man" of European letters. The former appellation indicates his far-reaching and encompassing knowledge and activities in the fields of comparative literature, philosophy, and the history of ideas; the latter characterizes the man, highly esteemed and beloved by his contemporaries, the men of letters of his generation in Europe and, after his emigration from Nazi Germany, his students and colleagues at institutions of higher learning in the United States.

When Rudolf Kayser joined the faculty of Brandeis University in the Fall of 1951, I at first stood in awe of the scholar and critic I had long known by reputation—as a living legend, almost—the man who had once been in the mainstream of German literature and had attended the premieres of many of the important German plays that are now part of world literature, who had personally known great literary figures like Thomas and Heinrich Mann, Hugo von Hofmannsthal, Gerhart Hauptmann, Alfred Döblin, Max Brod, Franz Kafka, Stefan Zweig, Arthur Schnitzler, Richard Beer-Hofmann, and Jakob Wassermann.* But I soon felt reassured by

---

*Once Kayser showed me a number of letters from some of these and other literary luminaries in which holes had been punched to make them fit ring binders. When I gently chided him for what I regarded as an act of disfigurement and desecration, he pointed out that the receipt of such letters was an everyday occurrence in the editorial office that he headed for a decade.

Kayser's personal warmth, his gentleness, and his unassuming attitude as a colleague, and in the course of time Rudolf Kayser became my dear fatherly friend.

In his first years at Brandeis, Rudolf Kayser taught philosophy as well as basic courses in Humanities that were devoted to a broad presentation of the cultural heritage of the West. When the rapid development of the newly founded university justified additional courses in German language and literature, Rudolf Kayser also taught his mother tongue and shared with his students a rich and uniquely personal experience of modern German literature. For a time he also served as acting librarian, making his bibliophile and bibliographic expertise available to the entire university community. Because this frail man displayed surprising vitality and a remarkably youthful outlook on life, he deeply enjoyed the personal relationship with gifted and appreciative students that is possible only at a small university. He was also stimulated by the close contact with such distinguished colleagues as Ludwig Lewisohn, Nahum Glatzer, and Simon Rawidowicz. Rudolf Kayser's retirement in 1957 as Brandeis University's first professor emeritus marked the end of what he often described as his happiest years in America.

Rudolf Kayser was born on November 28, 1889, at Parchim (Mecklenburg), the son of a Jewish leather merchant. When he was still a child, his parents moved to Berlin where Kayser attended secondary school. He then studied philology, literature, philosophy, and art history at the universities of Berlin, Munich, and Würzburg, taking his doctorate at the last-named institution in July of 1914.

For several years he taught German, history, and philosophy at various secondary schools and institutions of higher learning in Berlin. But he became increasingly active as an editor, essayist, critic, and anthologist, and began a long association with the renowned S. Fischer Verlag. From 1924 to 1933 Kayser was the editor-in-chief of Fischer's *Die Neue Rundschau*, the foremost cultural journal of Germany (and possibly Europe), to which the world's most distinguished writers and scholars regularly contributed. Having written for the expressionistic journal *Die Aktion* as early as 1911, Rudolf Kayser became a prolific writer, editor, and critic in the early postwar years. He edited works of J. G. Fichte, Wilhelm von Humboldt, Achim von Arnim, and Ludolf Wienbarg. *Verkündigung. Anthologie junger Lyrik*, the collection that Kayser edited in 1921, is widely regarded as one of the finest anthologies of expressionist poetry. In the same year Kayser's biblical legend *Moses Tod* appeared as a volume in *Der Jüngste Tag*, the Kurt Wolff Verlag's celebrated series of expressionistic literature. In 1923 Kayser published *Die Zeit ohne Mythos* (An Age without Myth), a profound assessment of the precarious ideological, sociological, and cultural situation of postwar Europe. *Das junge deutsche Drama*, published in 1926, is evidence of Kayser's enduring interest in the theater, as is his service as dramatic adviser to the Berlin *Volksbühne*. *Dichterköpfe* (Literary Portraits, 1930) contains two dozen tersely formulated but richly informative essays on great literary figures from Spinoza to Knut Hamsun. Kayser devoted full-length biographical studies to two of his subjects in that collection. *Stendhal*, subtitled "Das Leben eines Egotisten" (The Life of an Egotist), appeared in Berlin in 1928, in an American edition two years later in New York, and in Spanish translation in 1934. The book drew enthusiastic praise from men like Stefan Zweig, Thomas Mann, and Alfred Kerr; Heinrich Mann called it "the best example of a *vie romancée*." In his biography of Spinoza, perhaps his most important one, Kayser endeavored to give a "Portrait of a Spiritual Hero." The book was published in Vienna in 1932; an English translation, with an introduction by Albert Einstein, was issued in New York in 1946 and reprinted in 1968. In a book published in Vienna in 1934, Kayser concerned himself with the life, the work, and the age of Immanuel Kant. Kayser's book *The Life and Time of Yehudah Halevi* appeared in New York in 1949.

In his biographies Kayser does not deal primarily with the works of these great personalities but concerns himself more with their tragic life stories. The facts of their lives, often given in minute detail, and information derived from letters and documents are put together like a mosaic from which the works of Kayser's heroes emerge naturally and organically against the background of an epoch. Thus these factual biographies often read like romantic fiction. This technique is characteristic of Kayser's writings as well as of his lectures; he endeavored to present an individual and his work through the events of his life and against the background of his time.

In 1924 Rudolf Kayser married Albert Einstein's stepdaughter Ilse. The Kaysers' home on Nymphenburgerstrasse in Berlin soon became an international cultural center, though Kayser, who was essentially a conciliatory and mediating spirit, did not participate in the more turbulent literary currents of his time and kept aloof from fads and feuds. It is known to only a few that Rudolf Kayser wrote a biography of his famous father-in-law. The book was published in 1930 under the pseudonym Anton Reiser* by Albert and Charles Boni, New York, with a foreword by Einstein himself. In 1933, after the advent of the Hitler régime, the Kaysers were forced to emigrate to Holland, where Rudolf Kayser found employment with the publishing house A. W. Sijthoff in Leiden. However, in July 1934 Kayser had to suffer the tragedy of his wife's untimely death at the age of 36. His deeply moving memoir *Ilse: Ein Requiem* was privately printed in Holland in 1936.

By that time Rudolf Kayser was already living in the United States, where he had emigrated in 1935, settling in New York City. Soon after his arrival he became a lecturer in philosophy and the history of ideas at the New School for Social Research. From 1936 to 1951 he taught courses in German language and literature at Hunter College. During World War II Kayser also worked as a translator for the government's Office of Censorship, and in 1950 he prepared cultural programs broadcast by the Voice of America.

Following his retirement from Brandeis, Rudolf Kayser had to exchange the relative rusticity and tranquillity of Watertown, a Boston suburb, for life in Manhattan, which he had always found difficult. "I had imagined the fifth act of my life differently," he once told me. Yet the devoted care of Kayser's second wife, Eva, whom he had married in 1936, kept his last years from becoming elegiac or

---

*The protagonist (and title) of an eighteenth-century psychological novel by the German writer Karl Philipp Moritz.

anticlimactic. The Kaysers lived in a bright, airy apartment overlooking the George Washington Bridge, and the scholar enjoyed working in his book-lined study and taking walks along the banks of the Hudson River or to nearby Fort Tryon Park. Summers in New Hampshire and voyages to Europe and Israel brought Kayser relaxation as well as stirring encounters and reunions with persons and places. Despite an ailing heart and failing eyesight, Rudolf Kayser continued to be remarkably active. He resumed his teaching of courses in German literature and the Humanities at Hunter College on a part-time basis, gave numerous public lectures (particularly before the New York Association of Teachers of German, with which he had had a long relationship), and continued to contribute to a wide variety of scholarly journals and more popular periodicals and newspapers in this country and abroad. His last projects included articles for the *Encyclopaedia Judaica* and the *Lexikon des Judentums* as well as writings on French thinkers (a book entitled *Claude-Henri Graf Saint-Simon. Fürst der Armen* [Prince of Paupers] appeared posthumously in Munich in 1966), and on the philosophy of language.

In two works that were especially dear to his heart, Kayser returned to the literary form of the Jewish legend. In *Die Heiligen von Qumrân* he traced with great poetic vision the origin of the Dead Sea Scrolls and highlighted the clash of the three great religious and cultural spheres—Hebrew, Greek, and Roman—of ancient times. In *Hier bin ich!* God's age-old call to Abraham is transposed to an Eastern European ghetto and heard by a stunted, miserable boy. Unfortunately the little volume containing these stories, issued in Rothenburg ob der Tauber, did not arrive in New York until two weeks after Rudolf Kayser's death on February 6, 1964.

The Saints of Qumrân may be considered Rudolph Kayser's fictional swan song. The idea for this novella was born during a trip to Israel taken in 1961. His visit to the Hebrew University in Jerusalem brought him face to face, in a small room of the University Library, with the huge clay jars that contained the precious documents hidden about two thousand years ago and only accidentally discovered in the middle of the twentieth century. What Kayser felt at the sight of the scrolls (which at that time had not yet found their ultimate shelter in the building erected for them later through the generosity of American friends) he expressed in an unpublished account, written for relatives and friends, of his voyage to the land of the Fathers: "The most precious possession of the Library is the Dead Sea Scrolls. In America I had read as much as possible about this most magnificent discovery of our time. Now the Scrolls are before us in clear square script. Showcases hold the nobly molded clay jars in which the Essenes preserved their scriptures. My hands and eyes touch two thousand years. This is more than a curiosity; it is the awakening of the mythological age."

Back in the United States, the haunting memory of the Dead Sea Scrolls inspired a poetic vision of their origin. *The Saints of Qumrân* demonstrates once again the power and purity of Kayser's poetic language, his profound sense of history, his mastery in the presentation of his characters against the background of their times, and his deep religious feeling. The same passionate comprehension of man and his destiny, the same poetic observation of nature and man, and the same beautiful language characterize *The Death of Moses*, the legend that stands at the beginning of Kayser's literary career. *The Saints of Qumrân* (as well as *Here I Am!*, which is also based on a biblical motif) close the circle begun more than forty years earlier.

A few days after his last birthday, Rudolf Kayser wrote me: "The further dehumanization progresses, the more the ancestral heritage of our culture is crushed, the more do we, the survivors, need a community of heart and mind." An outstanding member of that community, Kayser strove to pass the humanistic heritage on to a younger generation so sorely beset by conflict and confusion, to make his voice heard through the din of an unfeeling space age. He was a man of true humility and quiet wisdom, and his buoyant, almost childlike optimism and abiding faith in the future permitted him to be serene and even-tempered even in adverse circumstances.

Only some of Kayser's short works of fiction and a modest selection from his essayistic oeuvre can be offered here. This volume is limited to Kayser's writings on Jewish themes, and these of course reflect only one aspect of his wide-ranging creativity, though a very important and characteristic one. Rudolf Kayser wore his learning lightly and wrote lucidly; his essays, like his lectures, are typically divided into clearly delineated sections and combine critical detachment with humanistic passion and the communicative fervor of a born teacher. It is to be hoped that this collection will draw renewed attention to an uncommonly rich literary and critical work and keep alive the memory of a rare human being.

Brandeis University HARRY ZOHN
Waltham, Massachusetts
April 1976

The Saints of Qumrân

PART I
Fiction

The Saints of Qumrân
A Story

Pliny the Elder, Flavius Josephus, and, in more recent times, Ernest Renan have reported that the religious sect of the Essenes, that is, the Sanctifiers, nested here and devoted themselves to the service of God and his law in a strictly regulated community. Pliny had called this sect stranger than all peoples of the world. Their life seemed to him as timeless and worldless as the mountains that surrounded them. The monks did not need the light and colors of the landscape, for they possessed the word, and the word is holy and rules over days and nights. The stillness that hangs over the cliffs was also in them, but their souls were not dead, but rather joyfully filled with the exultation of their knowledge.

I

The sky hangs over the Jordan Valley like a dark, wet cloth. Austere, hollowed cliffs plunge down to the shores of the Dead Sea, the sea—abysmal, luring, and horrifying like a sickness—that can be better surmised than seen. This ancient landscape, promising neither good fortune nor harm, is as mysterious and solemn as a prophecy. It prepares the observer for all the good and evil possibilities of the world. In all of history's violent changes it was sooner shunned than sought by its inhabitants. Only a few farms and villages indicate human settlements. The great roads that lead from Jericho and Hebron to Jerusalem make an anxious detour around the valley.

Since ancient times, shy men who flee from the sunlight have lived in the dark mountain caves. Here, in biblical days, David hid from Saul. Here, in all times, political refugees escaped imprisonment or persecution. Here, Bar-Kochba, son of the stars, planned his revolt against all-powerful Rome. And here, too, robbers and thieves sought refuge. Only the far-off bustle of life forces its way, like sunbeams, through the cracks of the caves. The profound stillness and dim, cheerless light rule, driving curious visitors away.

The pious Brothers of Qumrân had nothing to hide and nothing to lose. They belonged to this solitude, for the loud cities would have befouled their hearts. Sometimes single brothers appeared in the cliffs' gaps, looking as old, fissured, and motionless as the mountain walls. They glanced only fleetingly into the world and vanished again into the damp stillness of the caves.

Only the elderly Ephraim from Galilee appeared regularly in the late evening hours, looking wide around him, feeling the hazy, blurred horizon with his weak eyes. He was the gateman and guard of the monastery, and meditated in the night air outside his cell.

He spoke quietly to himself: "As yet the moon is not dipped in blood. As yet God has not chosen his anointed one, the Messiah; as yet Israel is not delivered. The Sons of Light must continue to suffer because of the Sons of Darkness, and the words of truth must rebel against those of falsehood. Faith is our weapon, the loyalty to our teacher our protection. Blessed be He in all His ways! God's will and word alone will drive the Kittim* into the sea. The Lord will decide when we will crush Belial** like pulp, and He will create a new union with His people. The cries of our hearts and the calls of our prayers reach Him better than a burnt offering or slaughtered sacrifice. Something great must happen, the destruction of the world or the coming of the Messiah."

Ephraim's thoughts built bridges between the mute life in the

---

*Tyrants
**Satan

solitude and the star-filled sky above the Jordan Valley. The murmuring of the praying monks sounded from within like the whispers of springs flowing over pebbles to the stream.

This whispered silence forced its way out of the mountain caves into the dark stillness. The first sun ray will pierce it. In the distance, the stamping of the legions, the roaring of the animals, and the cries of people herald the beginning of the day. Such awakening is not good in times of war and tumult. Anxious souls fear that all men will die of the wounds that God struck them for their sins.

Ephraim submerged once more into the darkness of his monastery and the silence of the Sons of Light. It had grown late, and the hour of the holy ablution had long since arrived. Again his examining eyes followed the mountain range. Then he, too, hurried into the washroom, donned the long white garments like those of the other brothers, and followed the procession of monks into the refectory. Each one sat on his designated stool according to a rank of precedence determined by age. Their heads were covered with knitted caps, out of which long, silver-white hair fell over the bowed faces.

They were all full of the experience of their community and the love of God. What could happen to them here? Man's evil did not affect them, for they themselves had to be good. They had understood the sense and salvation of life and found it incomprehensible that the world outside could be different from theirs. They did not want to abandon the world, as long as the world existed.

The Sons of Light piously awaited their Abbot, who was to them a priest, a father, a leader, a teacher. The small lamps on the table cast restless silhouettes on the bare, windowless walls. If the shadows moved, it was due only to the disquiet of expectation and the longing for the holy man, the center of their circle.

The monks had renounced all their earthly riches, had given the Brother Curator all their remaining small possessions. Every coin, every article of clothing, every piece of writing, and every past belonged to the community. The coins were piled high in the vaults. They depicted the heads of the strong men, from Alexander Janneus, who had had eight hundred pious Jews killed on the cross, to Pompey. The monks had left behind all knowledge of wives and children, of fathers and mothers. The world viewed that which separated them from such earthly things as rigid prison walls; but for them, it was a wall of protection against enmity, folly, hatred, and all the dark powers of Satan.

When the Teacher finally appeared in the doorway, whispers, like the crackle of an invisible flame, passed through the rows of Brothers. He silently stepped to his place and spread his arms, as if he wanted to embrace all of mankind and hug it to his heart. Gentle and radiant, he blessed the wine and bread, the seniors and novices of the community, and he blessed Israel; and each stood under the spell of the hour as if God himself were present. They then partook of the meager meal.

At the end of the meal, the Abbot lifted his voice to give thanks and praise to God. The old religious hymns resounded, their melodies entwining those gathered with God in bonds of love, as criminals are chained in imprisonment. They sang songs of praise and glory to God, but they also sang Maskills:*

> Yours, Oh God, is all knowledge,
> Yours are the works of justice
> And the secret of the truth,
> While men are the servants of falsehood and fraud.

And the boyish voices of the novices contrasted with the breaking voices of the elderly.

Then they all left the hall and went to rest, if they desired, or to study and meditate. But no one concerned himself with the nocturnal world outside.

The Teacher remained standing in front of Ephraim and eyed him questioningly.

"The moon and stars move in their regular orbits," Ephraim reported, "and are dipped in faded light. The noise from the streets is louder than usual during the day. It seems that new legions have come into the land."

---

*Songs of the wisdom of the Lord and the duties of man

"Did you hear animals howling in the mountains? Did you hear people in the villages calling for help?"

Ephraim shook his head, "No, Master, I did not hear anything, but I have further night duty today."

The Master bent down so close to Ephraim that their hair joined together as if woven in a bright carpet. He spoke softly: "Listen, Ephraim, I had a horrible dream about howling jackals and tigers that came from the ravine and sucked the blood from my veins like leeches. They mangled me, but in the reading hall they made a shy detour around the books. Do you believe, Ephraim, that God sent me a message of disaster? Must we help Him, in order that He help us?"

Ephraim did not know what to answer. With anxious eyes he met the other's face that held such a grievous expression as it had never held before. Then he spoke quietly, directed more to himself than to the Abbot: "I have no dreams; I sleep in peace and faith. It seems to me that both God and Satan are equally far from our hermitage. The moon shines so full and bright, the Saviour is still in the darkness of night."

He shrugged his shoulders and stepped outside once more for the last watch, until he, too, would be allowed to lie down. He saw the impenetrable darkness of the mountain-edged night. Only the weak illumination of the slopes broke through the world's slumber.

II

The next morning the Master appeared even more troubled and depressed than the night before. But he remained silent and admonished the Brothers to quietude and the performance of the daily pious activities. He sent them into the writing hall to copy the holy scrolls, or to their guard posts, and a few out into the country to bring the cloister vital provisions from the villages. Upon their return, these providers and scouts had to report all of their observations. They had seen frightened crowds of villagers and farmers muttering, listening, and sobbing, but the crowds dispersed when, in the distance, clouds of dust swept over the streets, or when the heavy marching of the legions loosened the tiles from the roofs. But they had not been seen themselves, since their approaching steps had frightened the people away. They remained the foreigners, the tyrants, unholy companions in the land of Israel, and even when they appeared to be friendly and good, a chasm of suspicion and hatred separated them from the sons of the land.

The Brothers of Light avoided mentioning the Princes of Darkness, although they had heard talk of them and feared the hour when they would discover their refuge. Especially Ephraim, who understood the foreigners' language, knew their deeds and crimes, their poets, teachers, gods, and laws. The state was all-important to them; they considered war and death the greatest good fortune. If one asked about their beliefs, Ephraim would answer, "They only have gods; we have God."

They seemed to respect the peculiarities, the God, and the way of life of the Jews, but in reality they despised them and awaited their destruction.

Timidly, a few of the novices asked, "Are these Romans the Shedim?* Will our blessed God send the Messiah to free us from them? When will the promise be fulfilled that a man from Judea will go forth and gain the entire earth as dominion for the one God?"

Those questioners had lived among the Brothers of Light only a short time. One was a sixteen-year-old, childlike in build and thoughts, who was, however, determined to travel the path of the Torah and Rabbis to the end. He had wandered far, from Samaria to Qumrân, abandoning his parents' home like a lamb eager to join the flock of the wise.

They called him Zechariah, the boy.

Ephraim could not ignore a child's plea for help. His words came slowly out of the cavern of his sunken mouth and gripped the hearts of the speaker and the listener. They were surrounded by a deep, summer stillness.

"Help," the old man began, "must come from yourself. Even the

---

*Demons of Satan

best, the truest laws can be a blessing only when you have recognized and understood their wisdom. Forget the existence of the outside world; live the life of your soul with pure, clean breath. We are cave dwellers forced to hide from the Kittim who want to destroy us and our laws. We are Essenes and have learned to smile when in pain. In our poverty we are rich, for we learn, learn unceasingly from the sacred writings of our people. God remains incomprehensible to mortals; we only perceive his presence and pray and cry to him in our distress. Do not forget, my son, the words of our leader Moses when God had made himself visible to him: 'I would not like to hear the voice of my God and see this great fire any longer, so that I shall not die.' "

Ephraim remained silent for many minutes before he continued, "God's love raises us over all mountains."

The motion of his hand declared that Ephraim's mountains extended to such heights that they encompassed the globe.

"And if they defeat us and make our country into a Roman province, that, too, is God's will. As long as we love Him, and smile when under pain, we are charmed against the Sons of Darkness." Ephraim's voice became stronger and louder for a short time: "Let them come here to our caves with their polished swords, their wild battle chariots, their golden insignias and deceitful talk—what can they do to us who are righteous and possess nothing! Let us think about the words of our prophet Habbakuk, that a just man will survive through his faith."

After this admonition he indicated with a weak gesture that his voice and thoughts had grown tired and that he wanted to be alone. He had nothing more to say. He wanted to guard the stillness like the breathing of a sleeping child.

III

Young Zechariah understood what lay before him and that he had to free himself from all temptations of evil and sacrifice the finite to the infinite.

He lived alone in a tiny, lightless cave with neither shadow nor sound. God had demanded that His people be holy, for God Himself is holy. Zechariah thought about this with an unrestrained gladness that neither weapons nor threats could destroy. He knew that he had been right in leaving the sheltered home of his childhood and fleeing to the Brothers of Light.

Zechariah had imbibed the elder's every word and idea, as if they had been beverages. His eyes that had glanced upon infinity looked back on the quiet happiness of his youth. He could not yet give up his memories, but he lived in the love of God, who was called *He who is*. Other gods are satisfied with animal sacrifices, but He who is demands more—He demands the human heart.

Zechariah had to wait until he reached twenty to be initiated into the religious order. He had to renounce forever all worldly pleasures, the possession of women and wealth, the use of weapons, hatred, ambition, and rebellion against oppressors. In humility and devotion he was to learn what God had revealed, and he was to walk in the ways of the law. He was still a child and knew of no other protection against life than that of pious submission. He had therefore traveled the long path from Samaria to Qumrân in order to join the flock of the wise.

Zechariah often accompanied the elderly Ephraim on his night duties. With impetuousness and perseverance, the child's questions closed in upon the wizened, frightened old man.

"Help me, my father, so that I shall not miss the righteous path."

Zechariah's memories flew through the small rooms of his childhood, through the modest farmhouse and passed over his parents' simple faces. He had loved his youngest sister the most, baby Rahel, whose little songs had always filled gardens and dreams. He had not been able to bid her farewell. Sobbing, trembling, and lonely, he had followed the voice of his heart into the great wide world. Rahel, delicate, singing little sister, submissive lambkin on the knees of her older siblings—what could have become of her?

In a dream, the prophecy of his life as a monk came to him. "Are dreams not the messengers of the Lord?" Are they not the Bath Kol* proclaiming His will? The child's gaze seared the old man's wrinkled face. Ephraim felt it burning, but he felt weak and tired in the face of this onrush and admonished him to practice humility and patience.

He spoke about almighty Rome and how it sought to annihilate the people of Israel through kindness and murder, through friendliness and sly machinations. The Romans robbed and stole, had stolen even the very name Judea and called the land the Syria of the Philistines, Syria Palestine, and they defiled the strict ritual of the fathers through their heathen customs. And Rome had a powerful ally: the division of the Jewish people. Only when the holiest of things was attacked by foreigners did the Jews unite in a powerful battalion of faith, forgetting their bickering and squabbles. When the governor Varus set his legions upon the Temple, the Jews forced them out with the power of arms and the fanatic vengefulness of the tortured. But the country became a Roman province, and the insignia of the imperial power appeared on all the streets. A temple was built to Augustus in Caesarea, as if he wanted to challenge the holy of holies in Jerusalem.

From Galilee the voices of uproar passed through the land, audible only to the knowing and brave. They were the Kannaim.** They were Sicarii who recognized none but God as ruler and did not fear death. The Emperor Gaius even wanted his statue erected in the Temple. But the scorn and zeal of the Jews did not let the blasphemy occur, and Gaius succumbed to the hand of a Roman assassin.

As the old man spoke, the boy's imagination spun out what he heard, envisioning the murder, the suffering, the insults. "Babel, Babel!" the child groaned softly, inaudible to Ephraim. Then Zechariah raised his voice and gaze in outrage, and he would have screamed aloud if Ephraim had not calmed him with his hand. "Why does the Lord punish us so terribly, allowing Sodom and Gomorrha

---

*The heavenly voice
**Zealots

to arise from the dead once more in the land of peace and the pious? Are our sins so great, my father?"

"Do not bicker with God, my child, we do not know His ways. He sets the course; through misfortune He prepares the Saviour's path."

Calmer and smaller in his despair, Zechariah asked, "Who will be the Messiah, the Anointed One, the Redeemer? When will he come?" A childlike hopefulness filled him: "Perhaps our Teacher is the Messiah, the Father of Light?" But then he hesitated: "He is so good, pure, and wise, but he is no man of action who could chase the Romans from this valley." His thoughts floated silently in space, picturing the body of a saviour who would fight, pray, teach, and liberate them. And he remembered a prophesy that a Brother had recently told him. He had said that the Messiah would first appear in the Roman camp and nurse and heal the wounds of the heathen warriors before he, poor and unknown, would bring the dominion of God to the land of Israel.

A white star glowed over the mountains and disappeared behind a black cloud. "The cloud has eaten the star, my father! Will Rome eat Jerusalem, too?"

Ephraim shook his head and admonished the boy to pray, because the hour had long since arrived.

But once again the hot storm burst forth from the boy's soul and forced words from his lips so dejected and wild that fear spilled from his pores as he heard the words and he wished he could have forced them back into his mouth.

"Father, do you believe that God has died?"

After a long, sorrowful pause, the calm, sure answer came from the old man's lips: "When God dies, the world dies."

IV

The child's visions penetrated Ephraim's dreams that night. They ripped a wide gap in the wall of his room, through which he could see. He saw the emperor's golden eagle fly toward the heavens and with his sharp yellow beak gnaw the moon, whose color was blood-red like the fire of burning roofs. In the midst of the confusion he heard a shrill voice scream, "Babel, Babel!" A donkey trotted slowly and quietly through the flames; high astride it was the Teacher dressed in his fluttering white holiday garb, and in his shadow, small as a bird in a swallow's nest, sat his disciple Zechariah. "I am safe in God," he cried to all sides in a high child's voice.

When Ephraim awoke, he had to wipe the dream from his memory as he did the sleep from the corner of his eyes. Noiselessly, his lips murmured the prayer, "God of our fathers, bless us with the threefold blessing of the law that your servant Moses recorded."

All the Brothers had already gone to their places of work when Ephraim stepped outside. He saw how the sun dipped the mountain edges in morning light, with which the eternal darkness of the river valley menacingly contrasted. Only soft, distant noises pierced the peaceful morning.

In vain the old man sought the Teacher, whom he wanted to interpret his dreams, but no one had seen him. They said he had submerged himself in prayer and meditation the entire morning, that is, he was invisible and inaccessible to all. Zechariah sat among the novices studying the scrolls, and he was so absorbed in their wisdom that no words or glances could have broken their spell.

The Teacher did not appear in the community of the Brothers of Light until the evening meal. His appearance had changed. His skin was pale and pallid like the chalky mountain walls. His fingers, lying gentle and calm on the bread in its earthen bowl before him, were as thin as silver pins, as streaks of light. His praying voice rang soft and clear like a bird's call.

No one dared speak to the Teacher, over whose ageless and majestic face spread an enigmatic smile. The monks tried to read his face as if the future were written upon it, but they did not understand the language of this strange smile. So most of them reverted to themselves and their own thoughts.

It looked as if the master's smile wanted to eliminate all the fears of the age, as if it wanted to kindle all loves. It embraced the monks, Israel, Rome, mankind, heaven, earth, and death. It was the smile of a knowledge that knew the truth and felt safe within it.

Only the young ones accepted this smile. Astounded, thankfully, and knowingly each one passed it to his neighbor like a secret gift. It transformed the childlike faces, growing stronger on its path over the novices' stools, so that, as it reached the end of the table, it had grown into a joyous laugh. An old monk dispelled the laughter with the serious admonition of Jesus ben Sirach: "Accept everything that is ordained over you, and in the vicissitudes of misery practice patience. For patience is tested in the fire, and men that are acceptable to God are tested in the crucible of misery. . . ."

Late in the evening, the Teacher quietly stepped outside. It was the night of the new moon, and a round, white disc strewed the valley with bright light, as if it were covered with a shroud. The Teacher looked up carefully, trying to discern a red illumination somewhere on the horizon, but the light remained white; it remained cold and motionless.

He then ripped apart his garment with both hands and exposed the white skin of his chest to the moonlight, as if he could absorb it like a drink or divine message. He silently returned to his cave through a narrow opening.

V

The Roman cohorts came the next morning. Dark clouds of smoke and noise rolled down the streets, climbed the cliffs, ran over the mountain ridges, and narrowed the sulfurous air. It seemed as if the mountains themselves had begun to wander and had bound the valley with iron chains. The animals started with wails and shrieks, seeking to escape the valley, and even the birds made their circles higher and higher as they flew over the mountain range.

The Brothers of Light closed every gap through which the light rays and voices could have penetrated. Praying, they gathered in the refectory, pressed close together and united by fear, love, and the raging pulse of expectation. But the noise subsided, the dark floods sank back into the riverbed from which they had flowed. At noon, with the first lightbeams, the great stillness penetrated the timorous cloister through the gently opened gaps. "They haven't found us! The wild animal raged by; his teeth did not destroy us!" the Brothers rejoiced. But there were also a few faint-hearted ones who asked, "Will the enemy not come again?"

And the enemy returned, returned the same evening. But it was neither a legion nor a troop. Neither battlewagons nor pounding soldiers disturbed the nocturnal stillness. Only a single Roman wormed his way through the sparse grass, slowly and carefully, like a brown reptile, and only raised himself to his full height when he reached Ephraim, who had kept the night watch. The latter gave a frightened cry, as if a snake had bitten his heel. Trembling, he eyed the massive body that rose, towerlike, before him.

He was a centurion, a captain of the tenth legion who had participated in the morning's expedition and was now supposed to search once more the uncanny gorges for possible hidden persons. He wore no armor, no arm nor leg plates, but bore only a short sword in his tunic. He was alone.

His gaze examined the old monk like a strange, exotic animal. Then he broke into a loud raucous laugh that was so fierce and ringing that it was heard in the innermost caves and made the monks tremble. He tugged the old man's white beard, turned him around like a puppet, raised his arms and lowered them again, all the while roaring, shrieking and snorting with laughter, so that his plump face flushed red and his muscles began to ache. The game lasted a long time and put the Roman into an increasingly cheerful mood. Ephraim remained motionless with a slight, gentle smile and an expression of diminishing fear.

When the centurion was finally tired of his foolishness, he devised another amusement designed to frighten the old man. With a resounding voice he insulted him and the entire Jewish people. He chose raw, ribald words on the assumption that the Hebrew would not understand. "Old rag dog, cursed Jew dung!! Here you hide in a stinking rathole that we will smoke out to the last man. Here you dare defy the emperor, dare deny the ruler of this wretched province, dare maliciously attack, plunder, and kill his officers and soldiers! You must be a leader of these robbers, these cutthroats, this murderous mob that slyly and cowardly keeps itself hidden. No one could find you, you Hebrew riff-raff, only *I* succeeded—I—a simple centurion from the Apennines whom a stupid commander sent into this disgusting, scorched valley that reeks of salt and sulfur like the three-headed Cerberus. The procurator, that old rascal Cessius Flavius, will praise me when I deliver this mob into his hands. Ha, will he be astounded!! What would you like as compensation, my brave centurion? Rome will pay you anything, Rome, powerful, rich Rome that possesses all the money in the world. Yes, it should pay me, rich, wild Rome. I will present my bill—a piece of gold with the emperor's picture for every Jewish lout. Now, centurion, go into the robbers' den! These rats, this groveling vermin will cringe at the sight of your Roman face, at the sound of your commands."

As he tried to force his way into the mountain crack behind Ephraim's back, the old man said in a clear, powerful, and simple tone, speaking the language of the Roman: "No, sir! No foreigner may enter this sanctuary. We are the Brothers of Light and live in the darkness of the poverty of this cave. If you were to stop pelting me with abuses, you could hear pious singing coming from it. It praises our God and begs for peace. Centurion, you live in light and luster, but you are still the Sons of Darkness."

Some time elapsed before the centurion could compose himself and speak. He had never, for a moment, considered that the old Jew could understand the language of the Romans and thereby also his ribald vulgarities that his mouth had spurted merely for his own amusement. The game was now thoroughly disgusting to him; a foul aftertaste lingered. His anger was therefore so much the greater that this miserable wretch dared bar his entrance to the cave. In blind fury he ripped out his short, double-edged sword, the metal of which reflected the white moonlight.

But Ephraim had pulled himself together; he no longer feared the raving barbarian. He walked up to him with small, mincing steps and said with simple calmness: "Hundreds of monks, all unarmed like myself, form a wall of protection around this sanctuary. If you were to kill us all, you would find neither treasures nor weapons inside, only poverty, peace, and books."

The centurion became somewhat gentler, but also more inquisitive.

"What do you do here? What ties you to such a miserable life?"

Ephraim noticed the beginning of a change in him and started to speak in a didactic voice, as if to an ignorant child: "Our oaths bind us, oaths that we will not break. They make our life seem hard and joyless to the observer who comes from the outside. But we feel differently; we are happy that we are permitted to serve and are not forced to rule."

The skin of the Roman's face was as leatherlike as a dark hide. Light and genial traces of thoughtfulness and gentleness appeared in the corners of his mouth and on his low forehead. What had touched him the most was the old man's language, this pure clear Latin which he himself spoke so awkwardly. He kept pondering: Who is this old man who speaks like a noble Roman? To what people, to what community does he belong? Is he a gnome or a fool, Rome's enemy or a hermit banished to this solitude by some strange law?

This curiosity engrossed him so much that he hardly heard the old man's words and almost forgot the purpose of his mission. But this word *oath* brought him to his senses and became the signal for him to question further.

"Oath? So you are conspirators against Rome! I knew it! To whom have you sworn and what do your oaths demand?"

"They demand peace, poverty, chastity, and the love of God and mankind."

"And I'm to believe that, you simpleton? One doesn't swear to such things, which one reads in stupid storybooks for women and children. Men laugh at that; they want to live, to fight, to spill blood and have women in their beds. And who demands these oaths?"

"We are two hundred Brothers of Light, Essenes, hermits who abandoned the world to fulfill God's laws. No one bears weapons, no one bears hatred."

"And I'm to believe that?" the Roman screamed. "I will kill you all, I, alone, with this sword. See how sharp it is! I could slice your mountains with it!"

After a pause he said, "Who is your commander? I want to see him."

And from the corners of Ephraim's mouth spread again his small, superior smile that lay around the soldier's arms like a heavy chain.

"You will not, for we have no commander. We follow our master, teacher, and priest. He is a saint, and in union with God and mankind."

The centurion attempted an obstinate grin, but it stuck in his features like a motionless sketch. Astonished, he shook his head.

"You call him your master; what ties you to him?"

"Our oath, we swore faithfulness to him . . ."

"We swear, too; we swear and curse, we hate, but we are also good and obedient to the Emperor. *Aut Caesar, aut nihil.** Tell me about your oaths, my old man. I find you indescribably droll."

He paused in order to think—something that he found quite difficult. He was still uncertain as to whether he was dealing with harmless fools or dangerous enemies of his lord, the mighty Basilius. His weak mind was incapable of deciding. It would have been easiest to slaughter the old man and everyone else who would oppose him. But then he would never find out about the mysterious oaths of which the old man had spoken. And for the first time in his life, the centurion was touched by compassion for another man, for this old man who had done nothing to him and who spoke to him so well and wisely.

The centurion was dissatisfied with himself that it was not possible for him to rely on his sword as he would otherwise have done. Instead, he had been overcome with the vexatious duty of thought. With long strides he paced to and fro, looked at the silent landscape and into Ephraim's observing face, and shook his large, plump head. He decided to question still further.

"Hm, yes, well, your oaths. So you are vassals, slaves, or serfs. I

---

*Either Caesar or nothing

do not understand the differences; I follow our emperor who despises you. Then, by all gods, whom do you follow? And your oaths . . ."

Ephraim answered calmly, "We follow our God and our conscience."

The centurion broke into his vulgar laughter again and, shrieking, slapped his fat thighs. The short span of uncertainty seemed to be over. Now he knew exactly what to make of this mountain miracle. He remembered that he had already heard about similar religious penitents, fools, and babblers in other parts of the realm. So he struck up his lofty, mocking tone again: "And who is this God, then, who demands such oaths? Is he like the emperor?"

And then something happened that Ephraim could never explain. In his soul he heard the holy words of the Scriptures, like an inspiration from heaven. He had to repeat them to the bewildered Roman, who could not understand these words, in the language of God.

"*Ehyeh asher ehyeh!*"

With raised arms he recited the three words in ecstasy, deep devotion, and emotion, totally removed from time and space. The words visibly intimidated the Roman like a terrible magic spell, so that, anxious and bewildered, he asked for a translation. Some time elapsed before Ephraim found the Latin words.

"I am He who is here. I am He who is." Then he turned to the centurion. "He is the one and only God. He is our ruler, our father, our liege lord. Praised be His name."

"Our gods are different, wild fellows like us. They eat, drink, fornicate, and anger us often, but they have power. One must be on one's guard with them, and offer them copious sacrifices."

But he did not continue; he gripped his sword, smoothed his tunic, and inspected his extremities, and gazed toward the heavens and earth as if he expected some terrible occurrence. The solemn Hebrew words that the old man had spoken in such ecstasy still resounded within him and awakened feelings of uneasiness, suspicion, and nausea.

Like so many primitive men, he was suspicious and superstitious. He knew of no weapon other than his sword, of no jurisdiction other than power. His knowledge thus limited and small, he was often gripped with mistrust and panicky fear when faced with the unknown or incomprehensible.

He was firmly convinced that the old Jew had cast a spell on him. He felt as though he had been whipped and wished he were far away, away with his own people.

This entire encounter with Ephraim had grown distasteful to him. He had to put an end to it, but he had to preserve his Roman honor.

"You are an old rat-tail; I don't trust any of you one step. I would love to crush you all with a loud smack; your old bones would go squish. I don't want to do it, at least not today, because you bear no weapons and speak my language so nicely. . . ."

But then he was at a loss as to what he should do, because he could not simply give up the attempt to enter the cloister. So he asked once more, but this time more out of embarrassment than out of curiosity: "Well, what have you sworn to your God?"

"That we love Him and mankind, that we do good and keep evil from our threshold."

VI

Ephraim also found this discussion annoying; it could not achieve anything. But the community was in very great danger, and just as great was Ephraim's longing to report to the monks and confer with the Master.

The centurion chattered on in confusion. He sought to vaunt his Roman divinities that were so much more understandable and powerful than this weird Hebrew God in whose name the old man had cast a spell on him. Childish and excited, he told about them.

"When they are angry, they torment and destroy us, our children, and children's children. Jupiter is the emperor; he defeated all the Titans and married the beautiful Juno, the mother of Mars, Vulcan, Hebe. . . . Oh, I am never sure of this family. The gods always quarrel among themselves, just like men. How is it with you, old Jew? Is your God a quarrelsome weapon-bearer, too?"

Ephraim suppressed a smile and the feeling of superiority in the face of this barbarian. He had to speak in his language and disguise the holy in unholy words in order to alleviate the danger threatening him and his Brothers.

"Yes, our God carries a sword; he fights against the guiles of the devil, the Prince of Darkness. We help him through our love, follow all the commandments, and overcome the temptations of evil. We must be truthful."

The centurion wanted to hear no more of that which he could not understand. Again he became mistrustful and rude. He screamed his suspicions at Ephraim: "Words, hollow words, craven words that are meant to cast spells on me. Shifty scoundrel! Show me your armories, you old lout, your swords, knives, projectiles. . . . I know that you are the cursed Sinari, the cutthroats, treacherous mountain bandits. Your big words do not fool me. Open your ratholes!"

When Ephraim remained silent and motionless, the centurion continued: "To be truthful! You mean we should not lie, although they lie to us and cheat us every step we take? Don't make me laugh! *Decipiatur mundus*, let the world be cheated. It does not want anything else. Even the gods, these old rascals, cheat and let themselves be corrupted with the delicious fragrance of sacrifices. Is it any different with you?"

When Ephraim persisted in his silence, the Roman roared: "If I were to stab you in your thin bones with this Roman knife, then you would quickly renounce all of your oaths, pledges, and magic words, this whole foolishness, wouldn't you? Don't I know you, you old rascal?"

Ephraim's smile had never been so cheerful and superior, and therefore so perplexing for the centurion. With an effort, the latter jumped up to reach a decision at last, but it did not yet come to him. In vain he contemplated everything and sought arguments that would lead to enlightenment.

"*Castus, puritas*, chastity, purity, what revolting words! Don't you lie between the thighs of your women and climb around on their breasts as you do on the mountains of your country? That's what your entire holiness is—only empty words and fat lies. You are long since ready for Pluto, for Hell!"

Then, suddenly, a thought occurred to him that seemed a lucky way out so that he could finally leave the place with soldierly honor.

He laid his raw, heavy hands on Ephraim's narrow shoulders. He spoke slowly and noticeably relieved. "I will let you live, you old frog. You are only a harmless word maker, no zealot, no cutthroat. You could have slaughtered me, you only needed to call out the other rats; you are many and I am alone. That was decent of you, old faun, old satyr. Perhaps you are really only a band of madmen, of poor men who don't even have enough money to erect a statue to your God, miserable wretches not worth a kick in the rear.

"But the procurator hates your people. He wants to destroy you all. He considers your talk of redemption, God's love, and chosenness dangerous to Rome's security. He wants to nail you to the cross, you wordy, headstrong fools who do not understand Rome and its advantages, which you could share. In Nazareth, Galilee, and Jerusalem the crosses grow out of the ground like forests and thereupon dangle all who have prattled as you have.

"You probably don't know, you old gnome, that there are such smart talkers who hang themselves on their idle talk everywhere in the world, in Rome, even in the army. They call themselves prophets, philosophers, teachers, and poets, and are nothing but vermin gnawing at great Rome. They imagine themselves to know more and be better than the gods themselves. The Greeks are the worst. They think they are the rulers of the world, these arrogant Hellenes, but Rome's fist has crushed them. Now they are nothing but paltry schoolmasters in our service; we are their good pupils when we can use them. But we are strict when they dare rebel against the emperor."

He shook his heavy head once more. "Strange, my old man, you are similar, you Jews and Hellenes. You believe in the word, in wisdom, love, and goodness, but your countries collapse like rubbish and your lands belong to us. Your philosophies are useless against the Roman legions. . . ."

Ephraim smiled at the soldier, whom he well understood and

liked. "Our wisdom! It is no secret knowledge, no magic; everyone who learns to believe in God and to follow Him and His commandments can have a part of it."

"Again only more words, wild talk, book babble! If he had power, your God, he would have chased us out of the country long ago. He is only an idol, so poor that he has no icon and no one brings him sacrifices. Just dumb talk, my old man. Where there is power you will find God, wisdom, and luck. Long live the emperor!

"Now listen. I am an old warrior, a soldier of the emperor who stole your land from you—which was his right, true? We want to exterminate you all, you mountain worms, and if we do not kill you right on the spot, you will hang on the cross; then you will say everything that the procurator wants to hear. I can't do anything for you but give you time to do something. Do you finally understand me, you old, dumb, bearded, white-haired circus hack? I will send you a Greek from my cohorts, a fool like you, who also thinks he's a pillar of wisdom and hates the sword. He is no Roman, he will never become one—he should find out what goes on in your caves, what the bawling you call prayer means. Be smart, old mountain rat, sly, not wise; do you understand me? *Carpe diem*, use the time! I won't say more to you, white-beard, or they will nail me to the cross, too. No one is safe today."

"Sly, not wise," Ephraim repeated softly as the Roman disappeared into the darkness of the valley and the crevice of the mountain wall opened to bring the old man back into the community of the pious.

"Maybe—no, even certainly—the Romans are slyer than we are," he thought, "these men of strong will, of monstrous deeds, the rulers of the world. But we have our God to protect from them; He is weaker than they are, because He is holy; He demands that we be as holy as He."

Only now did Ephraim feel the weakness of his frail body, that his limbs trembled like leaves and his gaze faltered. He had to lean against the mountain wall that threw back the white light of the starry heavens into the darkness. His thin, trembling hands stroked the chalk wall that separated him from his brothers, and this movement was at the same time a caress and a supplication. His tightly pressed lips murmured words of prayer.

Ephraim stepped back into the cave. His steps had hardly crossed the threshold when he began to reel and sank to his knees. A few novices caught him and carefully led him to his place in the refectory. The community was assembled there around the motionless Teacher. The Brothers bent their faces and bodies toward him, to protect him and trust him till the end. They knew that Ephraim had experienced something frightening and that the message he had for them could be deadly.

Anxious minutes of silence and his slow recovery elapsed before Ephraim could report in a thin, breathy voice, struggling for words and air.

"Sir, the disc of the moon is as white as fresh milk, no glare and no noise disturb the peace of night. But a messenger of the Kittim, a servant of Satan, was here. He has discovered our caves. We no longer have any protection other than that of the impenetrable God and your wisdom."

As he began to stagger once more, the Teacher's arms grabbed him and with delicate gentleness led him to his own seat, while he stood behind him like a pillar against which the old man could lean.

Then Ephraim quickly and faithfully reported his exchange of words with the centurion to the breathlessly listening Brotherhood. So a wild warrior is also a man? He could have killed us all, he alone, but he did not want it. Had he felt God's presence? Thus the monks exchanged views, looked at the Master's hands raised in the oil lamp's dim light, and heard his calm voice saying: "Do not fear, my Brothers. We are in God's hands, and we will follow him as we always have. We thank you, Brother Ephraim, for your courage and example. May the Lord bless you on your paths. And now rest in peace, my Brothers, in the protection of His angels."

VII

The days grew shorter; summer slowly made its way across the mountains to the sea. Once more it bathed the valley in meager colors, until a cold, one-toned darkness took control.

The Cloister of Qumrân remained unharmed; the noise of the wandering cohorts did not return. The monks performed their daily chores even more silently and zealously than before; they cleaned the cells and the writing and reading rooms, provided for the kitchen and for water, and spent their days in accordance with the beneficially severe rules of their order.

Will the Greek come as promised? Was the announcement seriously intended? Will the cohorts attack us to nail us to the cross? Will everything, perhaps, remain as it has been until now? All thoughts centered around these sorrowful questions. Ephraim looked into the night with especial attentiveness and alertness.

Suddenly one night the young Greek stood before him, as if he had sprung from the ground. He wore the armor of a Roman legionnaire, but his bronze helmet, breastplate, leg plates, and his sword were much too large and heavy for his youthful body. This warlike appearance was in great contrast to the youth's facial expression.

The old man and the young man examined each other with curiosity until Ephraim addressed him with a Greek greeting. That was not unusual in the age of Hellenism, for Greek culture was increasingly popular among the Jews, without destroying their holy heritage. So the stranger was surprised less by the words than by the old man's friendliness and gentleness.

With a sharpness in his bright voice that one noticed was false and affected, he snapped at the old man: "I come on orders of the Roman legion. You are under suspicion of hiding weapons to use against the occupation forces and of practicing a secret cult, of possessing magic books having the power to cast a spell upon every foreigner and to rob him of his fighting power. A centurion who succeeded in finding you in your hiding place was practically paralyzed by you through a magic Hebrew spell, so that I was instructed to search the premises thoroughly.

"You know my mission? You know that it is the procurator's will that you be nailed to the cross for all of these transgressions, until you make a complete confession?"

With his wise old birdlike eyes Ephraim had soon perceived that the youth thought differently from what he said. He also knew how unwillingly the young Greeks bore Roman authority and how strong their suppressed desire for rebellion was. This knowledge eased him, but he did not want to foster a premature hope. He wanted to proceed slowly, intelligently, and carefully.

He nodded seriously to show that he had understood every word and was appropriately concerned. Then he said in a slow and laborious Greek: "Serious accusations, horrible threats against us peaceful hermits who lead a pious life outside the world. Indeed, horrible accusations, terrible threats! But believe me, my young Greek, we are innocent; we have shown the emperor nothing but due respect and never undertaken anything that could threaten the freedom and authority of Rome."

Ephraim's respectable appearance and this simple, convincing speech made an impression on the youth and caused his answer to sound more hesitant and modest.

"I take note of your assurance. It is not my duty to believe or suspect it. My mission was ordered by my superiors, and I must carry it through."

Ephraim observed that the young man did not know exactly how he was to carry his mission through. A hidden compassion and the consciousness of his superiority gripped him. He turned to the soldier in almost amiable fashion.

"Yes, we would like to facilitate your mission; we will gladly give you all the information you demand. It is certainly in our interest to refute these terrible suspicions and to prove to you that we are not Rome's enemies but only peaceful Essenes. Do not hesitate to ask about everything. I swear by the name of God to tell you the pure truth about everything."

But the Greek had brought no questions with him, just the order to seize the secret scriptures of the Cloister. So he told the old man that he just wanted to see the scrolls preserved there.

"No, that can not be! And you, especially you who are a Greek, must understand this!

"Our holiest things, our belief, our souls are written on these papyrus scrolls. They contain no secret teachings, no magic spells, just prayers and revelations."

The resoluteness and assurance with which the old man spoke made an impression on the helpless youth. Should he gain entrance with his sword, peacefully negotiate, or return to the army camp with empty hands as the centurion had done, but with no excuses?

Ephraim made use of the silence and continued where he had left off.

"They are written in Hebrew. Pretend that they were Greek, were unknown manuscripts of Plato, Aristotle, Pythagoras . . . the profound wisdom of your people. Would you deliver them to your country's conquerors, who would use them for unholy, hostile purposes?"

Shocked and blushing in his bright, young face, the Greek said: "Never! No, I could not! I understand you well, my father, but understand me, too. What should I do? I am in their hands, they would crucify me—your enemies and mine. I know the Romans; they possess a wild power and the will to conquer the whole world."

He paced to and fro with short, regular steps like a captured animal. He had given up the imposed role, was himself again, and wished to unburden himself.

"Only a fat Roman head could concoct something like that. Athens and Jerusalem must stand together; we have better weapons than Rome. I will not betray you, as the centurion desires. He is half animal, crude and uneducated, but his heart is not bad; he is better than most others in this invading army."

Ephraim was astonished. "So you do not love those whom you serve?"

The Greek had sat down on a stone in a light, graceful pose, the kind we admire on many antique statues. Smiling, he invited Ephraim to sit beside him. The two men formed a strange but touching group—the white-bearded Hebrew in his bright, sacklike garb and the young Greek, who did not belong in this landscape and apparel of war. He tried to grasp Ephraim's hand and to ask for his trust, but Ephraim remained stiffly hesitant, for the answer to his question had not come.

"Old father," he whispered almost tenderly to Ephraim, "You could have been Greek, a teacher of Stoicism like Cleanthes or Chrysippos, who say that virtue is foremost, but is not possible without knowledge. Teach me, too, to be virtuous, not to hate, not to despise. These are vices, evils . . . ."

He mused, continuing after a short, thoughtful pause. "Strange old man, strange Jewish people. . . . But I have confidence in you, in your unknown God, and in your invisible fight against Rome. You cannot win—only die, but if you will die as you live, you will yet be the victors."

These words and the painful, sensitive, dreamy expression on the youth's face had bewildered Ephraim. What was he aiming at? It seemed to the old man that the hour was not appropriate for him to plunge into another man's misfortune, for his own burden weighed so heavily on his old shoulders.

The Greek must have guessed Ephraim's feelings. He shook his head lightly as if to calm himself. "Do not believe that I want to confess, that I need your advice or would even like to join your order. I am a Greek and shall remain true to my origin. I see you, see your mute defiance, understand and approve of it and know that you must die so that Rome can live. Hellas, too, had to die; now it is Judea's turn. I had not known it before, but since I met you, I know it for sure."

Snatches of this conversation had passed through the cave's hidden gaps, within the hearing range of the Brothers of Light. Those who understood Greek sought in vain to derive a definitive meaning, but only the prophecy of their destruction reverberated in their minds as a great fear. The other monks attempted to decipher the foreign words from their Brothers' faces.

Zechariah had been able to understand enough to know that the foreigner had not come as an enemy, but possessed a good feeling toward the Jewish people. Unnoticed, he crept outside and slowly neared the two, who did not see him; he crouched by Ephraim's feet.

Shrugging, the Greek turned once more toward the old man. "So my mission is ended before it has begun. What will happen to me—I don't know, I must endure it. But you, you are warned; try to defend yourselves. Should Jerusalem really follow the destiny of Athens?"

With awkwardly phrased, barely comprehensible Greek words, Zechariah ventured a question: "Why are you a Roman soldier?"

He received no answer, but the foreigner continued: "Hellas and Judea must die. They believe in the word, in wisdom, in the Light. Rome believes in the sword and in the authority of power. We are weaponless and hate war. We must die."

Zechariah again ventured a short sentence: "But you are young! I am also young and life is still ahead of us!"

In the meantime, several monks, old and young, had followed Zechariah's example and looked curiously at the stranger. He did not notice anyone else, only the venerable figure of Ephraim attracted his attention; his deep trust of the old man brought him to speak finally about himself.

He had kept his former sitting position, but his voice had changed. It was so soft, now practically a whisper, that the small group around him pressed close together in order to understand him. He looked at Ephraim, whose presence loosened his tongue like a magic power and removed him further and further from the hour's raw authority.

He repeated the dark warning: "Jerusalem will fall as Athens did. Beasts of prey are destroying us gentle protectors of wisdom. But the word will outlive us; don't you, too, believe that?"

A young Brother repeated the biblical prophecy in his language: "No oppressor shall seize you any longer, for I now keep My eyes open. Rejoice, daughter Zion, exult, daughter Israel!"

In a feverish excitement the Greek bent over to Ephraim and, word by word, sentence by sentence, brought forth his speech without heeding the others. A long dialogue continued, and signified more than the movement between two men.

"Why did I become a Roman soldier? Because I was forced to, with threats and blackmail; and they promised me gold and great honors, flattered my good appearance and my Hellenic education. These are enticements that one does not resist when one is young. True, my father?"

Ephraim disapproved of these excuses: "When our life is at stake, we must not ask what we will be given for it. We must not trade our conscience for compensation."

The Greek hesitantly agreed. "You are probably right, my father, and the teachers of the Stoics would probably consider my behavior sinful. Something impelled me—perhaps it was mostly fear—perhaps . . ."

"Where do you come from, stranger?"

"I come from Samos, a Greek island; my name is Peukestas. I am an orphan, with no siblings; I am all alone. Ever since my childhood days I have heard about poets and philosophers. I wanted to become like them, to abandon the world for the sake of eternal wisdom. Did you ever hear of Pythagoras?"

VIII

"Pythagoras was our island's greatest son; he knew everything about men and nature. Nothing was alien to him; he could comprehend and explain everything. He knew the whole world, Hellas, Rome, Egypt, Babylon . . ., he knew mathematics and astronomy. He could play the harp and sing old and new songs. He knew the soul is immortal and it changes our bodies, but in rebirth we will be punished for everything evil that we have previously done."

He looked around, saw Ephraim's attentive face, and continued with youthful enthusiasm.

"Do you know what numbers are?"

When Ephraim nodded, the Greek said: "No, father, you do not know, for everything is composed of numbers: Heaven and Earth, sounds, matter, men, states, lights, darknesses, movements, stars, suns—the entire cosmos is composed of numbers."

"And have you no gods, no faith?" Zechariah interjected hesitatingly.

"The gods of our poets—Rome has robbed us of them, too. We gladly let them have them. They are worthless, these creatures of

Homer and the other poets. Our God is the universe to which everything belongs. . . ."

More monks had stepped outside through the narrow gaps in the walls and joined the small group.

Peukestas continued: "We live on the threshold between destruction and resurrection, Hellas's death and its rebirth, which will come someday. Hellas cannot die; its philosophers and art belong to eternity."

"God is also eternal," Ephraim said. "He, too, cannot die."

The Greek repeated, "Have you ever heard of the wisdom of Pythagoras?" and without waiting for an answer, "He was the greatest son of our island; his knowledge reached across all oceans.

"So know that I belong to Pythagoras's school and have rejected all false gods, for I believe only in knowledge, in Logos, the savior of all peoples, the redeemer of the oppressed and the ill. Believe me, Hebrews, we all belong to the Cosmos, and the Cosmos is one and eternal. We, who are unfortunate in depravity, the depravity of matter, will enter the eternal spirit, the universe, good and purified from the transformations.

"We Pythagoreans, too, live in a community far from the world and close to God, exactly as you do. Our monastery is in Croton. We want to free life from the filth of materialism, and dissolve ourselves in the harmony of the spheres, in the eternal order of the Cosmos. Light and darkness, unity and plurality, finitude and infinity, man and woman, good and bad: our paths of destiny lead between these poles not protected by poetic duties but by our will to purity and eternity alone."

He remained silent for minutes and looked into the blue-black light of the sky; his eyes searched the valley to see whether anybody heard them.

"The divine Pythagoras and your pious wise men, they are more similar to each other than perhaps you realize. King Areios knew, and told your priest Onias, that the Spartans descended from Abraham. Aren't we brothers in thought and life? We should chase away the Roman devil and free ourselves from the curse of barbarism! Why don't we unite in the protection of wisdom?"

"Because our God, 'He who is', has forbidden us to carry weapons, because we are bound by strict oaths to a peaceful life of service," Ephraim answered coolly.

Peukestas mutely shook his blond head, from which he had long since removed his bronze helmet. "The Stoics think so too, but how will the world become better, how will the raw power ever be broken if we do not act? You are cave-dwellers, troglodytes; but come into the Light, as Plato taught, and fear your shadows on the cave walls!"

All the voices grew silent; the white mountains and the black valley were silent. Then Zechariah dared to shatter the dark stillness and said in awkward Greek, interspersed with Aramaic: "God will help, will send the Messiah, the Anointed One, to deliver us."

"But when, young man? In what eternity?"

"When the time is ripe, when our suffering has reached the end, when the moon is dipped in blood-red. It is a sin to anticipate God's thoughts and decisions."

Peukestas raised himself, donned his helmet, arranged his armor, and walked out into the night. After a few steps he turned around once more. "I will return; I want to help, my Hebrew Brothers!"

The night enclosed the valley in narrowing circles. Above the mountain edge there was a gray light that faded into the darkness of the cloudless sky. Faint bird cries came from an immeasurable distance, and the old man's tired eyes sensed the advancing darkness.

Conflicting thoughts strained the Brothers' faces like tautly pulled cloths. Zechariah turned to Ephraim, who was barely able to absorb his questions. "Was he not right, this Greek? What do we get for our patience? What reward can we expect?"

Again this word *reward* penetrated the old man, this detestable word of an impious world.

"An Essene demands no reward when he fulfills God's commands. He does not want to receive any compensation, neither in this world nor the next."

Then they, old Ephraim and the younger Brothers of Light, stepped back into the cool, dark cave, back into the protection of their faith.

IX

Only a few of the Brothers had waited for them; the rest, even the Teacher, had gone to sleep. Those returning had to inform these few about the strange visit and discussion with the young Greek. There were differences between Zechariah's account and that of Ephraim; as they spoke, the former stood in the center of the novices, and the latter, tired and worried, sat in a circle of a few monks. But everyone was united by great astonishment, mild hope, and a unifying smile of expectation.

"Hellas and Israel, it sounds like a miracle, or is it all just a fleeting, false whim, a nocturnal phantom that will disappear in the light of day?" the elder Brothers asked.

They were, for the most part, familiar with Greek philosophy and knew how close those principles were to their old faith and how far removed from it. True, Hellas had developed the wisdom of concepts to such a great degree as no other people had done. But it knew nothing of the truth of the soul, the contemplation of the mind, the divine message.

They considered taking the liberation of a people into one's own powerless hands an impious audacity, for the Messiah, the Redeemer, the Menachem* was prophesied. He will appear in the light of Good and Justice and will force the enemy from the land.

They had become skeptical about everything that stemmed from men; only in the holy wisdom of their God did they find peace. Still, in many Brothers, especially in the younger ones, the words of rebellion and hatred had kindled a spark. Why all this suffering, this constant fear and persecution, why war and brutality?

Ephraim gave the answer: "Think of the words of the Rabbi Jesus ben Sirach."

"Of which ones?"

The answer came with the tone of a psalm: "For, as gold is tested in the fire, those men who are approved by God are tested in the furnace of misery."

---

*Comforter

"And should the misery continue in all eternity until the end of the days and the world? When should the Messiah come, if not here and now?"

No one knew the answer to this burning question, for there is no answer. Such a question touches the future as much as the hereafter, and both defy the asker.

When Peukestas returned after a few days, everything was totally different.

He had removed the Roman armor and, so as to be inconspicuous, wore a bright woven doublet like that of the Jewish farmers who bring their products to the markets of Jerusalem and Damascus. He moved slowly and cautiously, feeling the mountain wall with his gaze and hands so as not to miss the crack that led into the Essenes' cave.

The thin, trembling glow, like the thin, trembling figure of Ephraim, showed him the place that he sought in the chalky mountain wall. It was much darker between the mountains than it had been at his first visit. A silvery cloud slid in front of the moon and forced the sparse trees into a blacker darkness.

The Greek's speech was disjointed: "Go away from here! Follow me to the palms over there, quick, on inconspicuous, silent feet. I am waiting for you. And come alone!"

The old man did not know what to make of this secretiveness, for no one had been expected to come out of the nightly darkness. He shook his bearded head, retreated into the cave for a short time to order another watchman, and followed the Greek through roundabout and secret paths.

The few crooked palm trees stood in the barren stone world like memories of a prettier stratum in the earth's history that had long since disappeared. The tiny shade that they supplied during the day was absorbed into the night that possessed but few motions and sounds.

The Greek had heard of a terrible disclosure that seemed to him as incomprehensible as it was ghastly. Even in this year of despair there were traitors in the Hebrew camp, who did not hesitate to deliver their countrymen to the Romans and their crosses. Holy fools, pious proclaimers had to die, for they preached revolt. The number of traitors is large, they are bribed by Rome.

"You, too, have been betrayed by one of your own. He is a miserable priest, a sworn enemy of the Essenes and your Master. He has disclosed the prophecy of your prophets to the procurator, that a man from Judea would go forth and destroy Rome, would win the dominion of the world. They want to kill him, the Menachem, the Rebel, the prophet, when they catch him."

A terrible fright came over Ephraim, who could not withstand the new onrush of Evil. After all, the threat was against the Messiah, the one sent by God, who, he hoped, could appear at any hour and would smooth the path to freedom in the bloody moonlight.

The Greek continued to report: "The procurator knows all about your cloister. The wretched priest has convinced him that your holy scriptures are magic books, the contents of which offers terrible weapons in the rebellion against Rome. He has sworn to get them and send them to Rome. There they will decipher and interpret them. There are many Hebrew traitors in the emperor's court." And with these words Peukestas disappeared into the dark that neither birds nor light beam enlivened, and left Ephraim alone in the still greater darkness of his fear.

Ephraim had heard that this procurator was fawningly devoted to the emperor, a wild lover of power and despiser of the Jews and Greeks. Everything that smacked of God and wisdom was, to him, a dangerous poison from which he had to protect Rome. Every book was to him a poisonous well, every temple an armory, every priest a venal magician. He had every sage, prophet, and renewer of faith nailed to the cross, the number of which grew so large that he had trouble procuring sufficient woodcutters.

Peukestas had stated the Pythagoreans' principle, "Friends have everything in common." He wanted to send notice when the Roman surge would begin. Then he would put a piece of papyrus with these five words under the palms on the eve of the danger.

"Where should we go? No paths lead to nothing," Ephraim had stammered. To this dark question the Greek had given a still darker answer: "Nothing exists just as well as something."

X

A chasm of fear destroyed the ground on which the Brothers of Light had lived so long. Would it swallow them all up?

For the first time, even the Teacher lost his composure. He called all the Brothers together, revealed the situation to them, and confessed that he could find no way out. Bloodshed, expulsion, and murder—this would be the future that awaited them.

But then his faith returned and spread over everyone who quietly prayed and would not have dared utter a sound of despair.

"May God's will be done, we shall submit ourselves to His holy decisions. May His presence accompany us through every awaiting agony."

And the Teacher commanded the lots to be cast in order to divine God's will.

Urim and Tummim, light and innocence, guilt and darkness: man is dual, existence is duality; yesterday as today, only the Law is one and eternal.

And the lots were cast.

God did not respond but hung like an ominous cloud over the future, and the night remained dark and bleak. Only He is wise, His silence a terrible punishment of the audacious who wanted to fathom His will.

At the evening meal the Teacher had totally withdrawn within himself. As always, he had blessed the bread and wine, but he paid no attention to the Brothers, neither to those who sat next to him nor to the distant, tender gazes of the young.

Then it came over him like an illumination. Tears streamed over his pale, darkened face, but he pulled himself together to announce his vision.

And he spoke with words that rang harsh and sharp; he spoke of the coming destruction of the Temple of God, of the expulsion of the sons and daughters of Israel from the land that Moses had opened to them. The emperor would drag them across the forum with scorn and ridicule, would sell them as slaves to all the world, and would triumph loudly because the last, the most resistant, the most uncanny of all of Rome's enemies would have disappeared from the earth.

After a few days, Ephraim found the arranged note under the palms. He swallowed his last smile and brought the small strip to the Teacher, the Master.

"Friends have everything in common."

Now they knew for certain and prepared the departure.

Perhaps the Messiah would still appear and lead them, as Moses once did. Perhaps their deaths would be the redemption that God had determined for them. Who could say?

The cloister's property, the coins and objects that the Brothers had brought with them were evenly divided. No one received more nor less than the other. Each one stood with a small bundle at his feet awaiting the Master's instructions.

Only Ephraim remained behind.

He lay on the ground gasping and staring, a dying man whom many called fortunate, for the last hour of his life was also that of the cloister's. When God's plantation was closing its gates, what good was this one withered stem?

The Master sat by his side, dried the sweat on his hot forehead and spoke words of comfort and piety. He had received Ephraim's confession of sin. It was as small, humble, and moving as his whole life had been. Then a soft, pure sigh carried a ninety-year-old life into the great silence beyond.

They buried him in the white chalky earth and turned his head toward Jerusalem, toward God's Temple, which the Roman axes would soon destroy. But the enemies did not know that out of the desecrated sanctuary the spirit would arise and expand into a great sky over the suffering world.

The Brothers had carefully safeguarded everything that could outlive the future. The cisterns that held the purifying, baptismal water were closed with heavy rocks. Like children, like invalids, they rolled the holy scrolls in strong coverings of leather and copper and lowered them with tender care into deep clay vessels that were sealed and caressed with tears and soft hands. Then they put them back in the niches of the reading-room walls.

Only the psalm-singing voices of the novices penetrated the melancholy stillness. The elders had to be silent, for the pain sat in their throats and obstructed every sound.

The Teacher, the Sage, the Father remained as the last protection of the divine colony, as the guardian of the dead and as the human sacrifice on the altar of history. He plastered and cemented all the cracks of the bright walls. The mountain that had harbored community, wisdom, and prophecy closed for eternal times. No Roman would find that which he seeks and for which his heart is not ready.

The Master stood silent and unbowed by the burden of the hour between the ageless mountains. Let them come and nail him to the cross, drag him across the forum in a triumphal procession, or throw him into the arena with wild animals: the work was done, the mountain locked; God alone had the key.

So the spirit remained, preserved mute and forgotten in holy scrolls in the dead mountain, on whose peak the Romans later erected a strong fort to terrify and threaten the oppressed Hebrew people.

In the year 1947 the bold stone's throw of a Bedouin opened the cave of the Saints of Qumrân and their secret to a world that was astonished and deeply moved.

(translated by Tali Perlman)

The Death of Moses
A Legend

And the Lord said unto him: "This is the land which I swore unto Abraham, unto Isaac, and unto Jacob, saying: I will give it unto thy seed; I have caused thee to see it with thine eyes, but thou shalt not go over thither."
So Moses, the servant of the Lord, died there in the Land of Moab, according to the word of the Lord.

Deut. 34: 4-5

It was late evening when they pitched the camp. Weariness and the exertions of the past days quickly cast the people into their tanned tents. Curses, mothers' cries of pain, and children's wails still floated in the air, only to sink into the star-filled night. The morning drew golden spires on the tents, which slowly opened, one after the other. Gaunt men, whose bodies were the mere expressions of hunger and despair, stepped out of the tents; they looked after the herds and poured water into small wooden vessels from the few hoses that were still filled.

Suddenly a cry broke through the camp still stretched in slumber—a cry sounding clear as the tone of the Shofar that swept before the Ark of the Covenant and as ardent as children's carefree laughter.

The seventeen-year-old son of the priest Joseph of Levi, Jobab, who every morning washed himself with scorched desert sand, had sounded the cry. People rushed to him from every side. Even the tents of the camp's edge had opened. Men and women flocked to him; the very old and the very young shuffled slowly behind.

Jobab stood on a rock, now totally bathed in the morning light. His brown eyes stared transfixed into the distance. All eyes were on his slightly opened mouth, over which a playful laugh began to spread. Finally he pointed toward the east, toward the brightly glowing horizon.

And then the sharp eyes of the young perceived that at the place where the world appeared to end the desert began to rise, undulating. The earth rose like someone who after a good night's sleep slowly pushes away his blanket and piles it at the foot of his bed; and the higher the sun rose into the new day, the stronger, wider, and more jagged the mound of earth appeared to rise. A soft wind blew over the sand, driving the grains toward the strange miracle.

Then the girls and boys threw their small bodies onto the desert ground and, with fear in their throats and repressed sobs in their voices, they called out the name of God to the earthen towers three times. The elders only smiled. They looked at each other joyfully, reached out their hard hands, and gently lifted the children up.

They knew that that undulating wall was not the Throne of God. They remembered Egypt, and the broad, massive mountains that protected the luxuriant land from the desert. And on their lips they formed the unaccustomed word *mountain,* and they pronounced it slowly and solemnly.

And the mountain began to grow. The last clouds fell from its peaks. In the brownish light of full day it stretched to an infinite distance. Everyone understood that the desert ended here. The long wandering, during which generations had died and been born, had reached its goal. Beyond this wall began promise and good fortune, the Canaanite paradise to which Yahweh had promised to lead his people back.

And an endless jubilation broke out in the camp. Shawms, drums, and shofars were sounded. Everyone left the tents. Even the sick and dying dragged themselves out of the camp to see the end of Israel's sorrow. New songs were born in the alleys and squares and were sung by all. Young people came together here, ripped the dilapidated rags of their clothing from their bodies, and began jubilant dances. Couples fell into loving embraces. Curses, bitterness, and misery were replaced by cheerful gestures and joyous words.

They called out facts about the mountain that no one believed. Each person knew precisely how high and wide it supposedly was and how much longer they had to travel to reach its foot. In a few groups gesticulating men even seemed to start fighting over it.

When midday came, the people already found themselves more open to new expectations. The conversations concerned the pleasures and benefits of the rich land they would enter in a few days. No one mentioned the forty years of privation and sorrow. But the desert radiated its painful beauty like a memory.

Like thoughts reaching to infinity, the desert's monotony stretched far into the distance. There was the vast, brown, endless sea through which led the tracks of a wandering people like a small rivulet. There was the deep, heavy stillness, which only jackals and divine promise could break. There was the beauty of distance, purity, and solitude. Gray swatches of clouds hung over the landscape like words of farewell.

A few boys had strayed from the tents, lain down on an erratic cliff, and now gazed silently down at the desert. These boys, who had been born and raised in the desert, who had spent their young lives between the pitching and striking of the tents, for whom quiet, strenuous wandering and faith in God and Israel's future had become the only substance of their lives—these boys had so filled their souls with the landscape that separation seemed impossible. The stillness was as much in them as they were in the stillness.

One of them extended his hands over the desert as if in blessing, and then let them slowly sink.

And then everyone began to pray. The hot, heavy air sucked up their words and sensations as scorched sand absorbs water. Their clear voices swelled, rejoiced, lamented, and yearned. Something was going on within them that they could not articulate.

Silently, they looked at one another. They knew that what was happening now was different from and greater than the separation between past and future. Decisions faced them, almost too difficult for their weak and helpless youth. The fate of the world was trying to consummate itself through them. Feelings so powerful, so deep and terrible welled up inside them that their bodies shuddered as if covered by frost. They could not push the past away from them. It was more than misery and deprivation to them; it was a sorrow that was deep and responsible, and laid bare their innermost being.

Finally one of them spoke. "It is not good to rejoice because we are leaving the desert. The desert is beautiful."

"Yes, it is beautiful," the others cried out and bowed low over the landscape, as if over the body of a beloved. They sensed that the wandering, the lack of every pleasure, the passing of the days in endless uniformity had ennobled them; hence they were different from those who had known the riches of Egypt and hoped to find them again in Canaan. They had consecrated their lives to none but God. Holiness burned in their blood. Knowledge guided their will, which longed for far more than earthly possessions. Faith bound them to one another in a community that was felt but never named and that had only one goal: God.

When they returned to the camp, the tents were being dismantled. The last part of the great wandering was to begin.

Another three days and three nights the people had to move through the desert before they reached the foot of the mountains. While encamped there, they lived totally in their imaginings of what awaited Israel on the mountains' far side. They exaggerated Egypt's splendors to a fantastic wealth of gifts, joy, and beauty, and they filled their souls so full of these dreams that they grew weary, bending over like overloaded grapevines. Desire gleamed on their faces and made them hostile and cunning. Their eyes sought to rob their brothers of the plans in order to keep all the benefits of the blessed land to themselves. And so they became greedy, quarrelsome, and petty. They called out abuses and boastings to one another.

"I will have the largest pastures on the River Jordan, with herds of cattle, sheep, and goats as innumerable as the herds of Abraham the patriarch. But you, you will live in the city, in a narrow, filthy room, and will barely support yourself with your wretched trade."

"And you will beg at my door, and I will whip you like a mangy dog."

"I will have a trade firm that will send caravans to Babylon, Damascus, and Cairo."

"I will accumulate gold, glistening, yellow gold. And my gold will be as high as a mountain higher than the Lebanon, and when I die, I'll take my gold and throw it in the Jordan, so that no one will have it after me."

The deprivations of their lives to this point manifested themselves in such wishes. Their hearts had grown hard and closed, and where help and goodness had once been, envy and distrust now ruled. They stood in the shadow of future possessions and were vain and evil. They stopped complaining, but they also stopped praying; they dreamed and schemed as robbers and conquerors do.

The last evening in the desert had arrived. The Israelites rested before their camp fires and talked, quarreled, and got excited. Suddenly, stony and large, their leader Moses appeared among them. His broad body was like a bridge stretched between heaven and earth, and his gaze penetrated into every soul.

The conversations were quickly silenced. They tried to hide the evil words and looks as a thief hides stolen goods under his clothing. A great fearful silence hung under the night sky.

"Leader, speak!"

Moses gestured, but still did not speak. His face expressed profound clarity and solemnity. He turned to the people, the mountains, and the desert, and everyone saw that an experience swelled his soul that was as momentous and moving as it had once been on Mount Sinai. And some remembered Moses' looks and words when he broke the tablets after the people had become apostates. Fear and shame gripped them. Many felt remorse, many feared the coming reproaches, for Moses knew every sin.

They formed a large circle. The poisonous greed had quickly vanished. Their faces showed humility and solemnity. All felt their chosenness by God, their community, and loneliness among the nations.

Moses stepped into the center of the circle. Slowly and dreamlike the first words resounded, and then they came rushing out in a mighty crescendo. And yet no word of reproach was spoken.

"Blessings upon you, O people of Israel, on reaching the end of your wandering. The sun will rise and set two more times, and then your feet will step on the bountiful land that Yahweh, your God, has promised you. Your herds will graze on home pasture, fountains will flow in your villages, each man will pursue his trade. Thus you will find peace and joy. God, too, will find peace, and His Ark will stand behind temple walls. For forty years I have led you through desert and deprivation, as God commanded. Now we are at the end. Yahweh's blessing will guide you further.

"I have seen the land of your children. The sun shines over pastures and lakes. Forests stand deep and dark. The sea gleams in the west. The seasons bring blossoms, fruit, and harvest. Eternal becoming and passing away surrounds Israel, and you will remain, my settled people.

"But my time has come. The Lord's hands are digging my grave in the mountains. You will move into the land of pastures and green meadows. Yet God's word will weigh like iron upon you. You were chosen from among all the peoples of the earth to know and proclaim the holy Spirit. Nevertheless, treachery will dwell among you, and the Lord's anger, enflamed by your unfaithfulness, will punish you and disperse you to all lands.

"You, Joshua, son of Nun, God has chosen henceforth to be the leader of this people. May insight illuminate your path. May sorrow and despair remain far removed from you until you, too, are called away by God from the burgeoning banks of the Jordan to His eternal Kingdom."

These words made an entire people tremble. Parting, admonition, and fate spoke, binding man to man, giving their lives breadth, uncertainty, and distress.

Brother, sister, the hour, the land, and God!

All secrets faded, wishes died, images succeeded one another. Memories welled up, fears convulsed their hearts, voices wailed, and everything pulsed together in this one realization, more improbable than the end of the world and miracles: the leader is dying!

There is no room for another feeling, there is no time for other thoughts; there is only this moment—vast, obscure, and dangerous, and in its center there is this one figure: heavy, erect, alone, the focus of a thousand glances, a tower above the desert, a man above the people.

A silence prevailed, stopping blood-flow and breath. In this crouching, lying, and waiting of the thousands, there were once more holiness, humility, and sorrow.

Is that our goal?

We wanderers, poor men, God-bearers at the gate of Paradise. We brown animals of the desert, gaunt, driven and led by God, chosen from among all the peoples of the earth. Fruit, pastures, milk and honey await us, a blessed land. But the leader no longer walks before us, no longer smooths our path, no longer lets Yahweh's words resound through mountains, valleys, and foes. We are the abandoned, the fissured tablets of proclamation, bleating herds, weighed down and crushed by the bloody burden of our God.

Harsh red evening on the border of Africa and Asia. A musty west wind swept stones and sounds into the camp, rattled over the tents, and lay down, calmed and caressing, at Moses' feet.

A dull roar emanated from Mount Pisgah. Clouds of dust flew about, stars darkened, and the atmosphere became dense. Amidst thunder and lightning a bright column of light appeared between the mountains. A great gleaming arm dug into the earth like a powerful shovel, lifting one clod after another and piling them up in endless pyramids to form new mountains.

This is how Yahweh dug Moses' grave.

Everyone looked up, filled with naked horror. They trembled and grew small and still before the awesomeness of God as if death, sickness, or curse were to befall everyone. Their eyes reflected terror and bewilderment.

When the first clods of earth rose and fell, Moses' body started to tremble. The reaction to this was shrill howling from those lying next to him, and this continued as muffled sobbing up to the outermost edge of the camp. Then certainty and faith returned to Moses, who stood up erect; surrounded by a bright glow of white hair, his face reflected smiles and joy.

Suddenly a group of boys rushed to him, embraced his knees, kissed his robe, and lay down, surrounding him like a luminous glow. Searching and clinging, they formed a circle around this powerful center. The camp was embraced by a silence that awaited a sign or word that would remove the intolerableness of the moment. God's hand continued resounding from the mountains.

Then Jobab, who lay supine at Moses' feet, jumped and steadied himself by clinging to Moses. The thin, trembling Jobab grasped his hand and spoke: "Stay with us, our leader. Do not die. We will return to the desert so that you may live."

Moses shook violently. As if overcome by fever he turned around and stretched his trembling arms toward the children; he was now an old man, his white locks blown by the wind. Then he grabbed Jobab's hands, looked him searchingly in the eyes, and finally laid his right hand on the youth's brown hair.

His words were so soft that only Jobab could hear them, even though the others pushed in close to the two.

"Boy, why has God chosen you to know the secret of my death? How is it that you, and only you, know the meaning of our wandering? This people is entering Canaan the way it left Egypt: vain about external goods, greedy for possessions and pleasure, strangers to Yahweh and His word.

"Israel should be glorious above all others. Spirit and service were the meaning of privation and death, of the long journey through Sinai's sand. Canaan should be the goal—not as paradise, good fortune, pasture, and wealth, but as settlement and homeland.

"God has not answered my prayer. They did not become free and kind. God's hope is destroyed, and I became hollow and dispirited. This is why God led me to Mount Nebo, pointed out the lands of Gilead, Ephraim, Manasse, and Judah to me and said, 'This is the land which I swore unto Abraham, unto Isaac, and unto Jacob, saying: I will give it unto thy seed; I have caused thee to see it with thine eyes, but thou shalt not go over thither.'

"So let me die, for my life is lost. Be true to God and your people. Sinai will return!"

Jobab was crushed. Tears filled his eyes. Pain pierced him, meaningless, incomprehensible, all the misery of life was foreshadowed in an instant. His body became so weary that he had to lie down, naked on the naked earth. Memories, hopes, wailing, and woe moved through his soul. The voices of the worried men and women who were watching him engulfed him like a stream of water in the distance. Sighing sadly like a person waking up, he stretched his limbs, raised his eyes, and, poking his finger in the sand, he lightly ground the dust. Dismayed, he jumped up and turned his face to the leader once more.

"I do not want to go to Canaan. I hate the land. I want to die in the desert . . ."

Angry looks engulfed him. Rage and shock engendered violent words about the blasphemer. But no one managed to drop his clenched fists or to invoke God's curse.

For Jobab had jumped up. The slender boy stood before them all on a rock. The east glowed in his eyes and made his face appear bright and deep. He spoke with a clear voice: "Brothers and sisters, look at the desert. Look at its brownness. Mimosas and thistles thrive in it. With nimble hoofs antelopes chase over it, the dust flashing like lightning. Columns of sand rush before the storms.

"In this desert we became a people. There occurred miracles, the like of which no other people has experienced. The bitter waters of Marah became sweet. In Sin quail and manna rained from the heavens, and in Raphidim we thirstily drank from rocks. From Sinai the Law resounded, allowing us to grow greater than animals and every race of man; we saw Yahweh's tablets and Moses' radiant countenance. There in the desert, in misery and stillness, we built

Yahweh's house out of acacias, lamb pelts, and purple, as the law commanded.

"Should all this be behind us like a psalm we have finished singing? Will miracles never again befall us? Will we never again be a united people, devoted to God and shunning earthly vanity? I believe we are leaving paradise as we enter it.

"Friends, we are like the desert, still and solitary, infinity around us and within us. Do you want to enliven the stillness with noise? Should market booths stand before the Holy Ark and bargaining drown out the priests' prayers? Do we want to feast on earthly goods, but renounce the Spirit? Listen to me.

"We will lose God.

"We were servants and will be rulers, satiated with wealth and pleasure, a noisy, clamorous crowd.

"We have wandered and are now supposed to be settled? We wanted to seek Yahweh and are now to find filled granaries, pastures, and contemplative evenings by the banks of the Jordan.

"We had misery and are now dripping with good fortune.

"People, let us return to the desert. Let us surrender to breadth and humility. Let us take leave of the good fortune that we have not yet enjoyed.

"Canaan is plague, rubbish, and filth. Its fields and meadows are sewers and breeding grounds of disease. Its gentle Jordan banks are as lascivious as a prostitute's breasts; filth and base lust prevail everywhere.

"This is paradise!"

The group had listened shuddering.

Did the mountains not collapse on the slanderer? Did the earth not devour him like Korah and his band?

But nothing happened. Moses, too, said nothing, but gazed at the young boy for a long time. His eyes conveyed neither punishment nor hate. But the people grumbled and demanded the death of the heretic.

"You child of the desert, begotten by jackals, you are no son of Israel."

"Stone him!"

"Stone him!"

This was shouted as more and more people crowded around Jobab, who stood next to Moses. Then Moses raised his hand. A thousand fists clenched the stones to smash the boy. But a look of pain and anger met them. Then Moses said slowly and clearly, "Do not kill him. For this child is holy and filled with God's Spirit."

Horror burned in every face. Unbounded astonishment stifled every sound and every movement. Confusion threatened everyone's thoughts and beliefs.

From the center of the group a piercing laugh broke out. It stopped only when Moses' glance met the old man who was sneering contemptuously.

Jobab had pressed close to Moses and now began to leave the camp with him. They climbed up to the mountains; their silhouettes were slowly lost in the jagged rocks. They stopped on a terrace and looked back at the praying people. Then Moses raised his hands once more and spoke the ancient blessings over Israel in a voice that rumbled like thunder over the desert.

He gave Jobab the command to leave him now, for the place where God had dug his grave was near. Then he walked into a crevice in the cliff, lost forever to human eyes.

Shaking with infinite pain, Jobab hesitatingly started on his way back. From a ledge he saw the Israelites' camp, from which loud voices and curses resounded. On the other side rested the desert, white from the shining stars.

Then Jobab threw his arms in the air, uttered a joyous cry and, kicking rocks before him, ran into the desert breathless and filled with the joy of homecoming.

The next morning the Israelites dismantled their tents, climbed up the mountains and down on the other side, and took possession of the Canaanite land.

(translated by Tali Perlman)

Here Am I!
A Story

And the angel of the Lord called unto him out of heaven, and said, Abraham, Abraham: and he said, Here am I. (Genesis 22:11.)

In those bygone days before technical means of transportation moved human settlements close together, even the smallest and poorest towns had their own physiognomies and strove anxiously to preserve their individualities.

In the wide, sparsely settled plains of the East, villages and towns were separated by hours of travel. Like lonely islands they floated on an ocean of flatland. During the winter they were closed in by great wastes of snow whose horizons blended with the gray, lackluster sky. Homes and steeples reached up out of the white plains like small black dots. If people did venture to travel the gutted roads, it was like a slow, heavy dark crawling through the vast gleaming whiteness.

Poverty was at home in these small hamlets of the East. The busy world of the great cities and the rich estates knew nothing of them. If their inhabitants were mentioned at all, a scornful smile appeared on the lips of the fortunate, who cared nothing for their need and for their bleak, joyless existence. They withdrew from the shadows of mourning and despair. Derision and disinterest were their armor against the gloomy image of poverty. And many among them hated the very memory of that darkness out of which they had themselves one day climbed into light.

The most despised and forgotten of these places were those inhabited by Jews. All eyes were closed to the black shapes of suffering and gloom. The pale faces of children and bearded elders must not be allowed to disturb the charmed circle of a brighter existence.

And yet these poor harbored no desire to attack the rich—they knew no hatred or envy. They were proud, in fact, of the hard life they had led through a thousand years under the shield of the ancient laws of their fathers. They had remained pious and humble and did not complain of their fate.

These Eastern village Jews were mostly tradesmen, mechanics, innkeepers, and laborers. Very few owned any land. They hardly knew that they were in the midst of a mighty empire. Their life was strictly regulated; it flowed between the banks of morning prayer and evening prayer, in eternal sameness. One generation lived like the next, and time brought only minor changes. Sabbaths and holy days shed the only light and cheer.

When the day's work was done, the young fellows gathered in the market places. They spoke of their business and their plans and often contrived elaborate pranks to scatter the humdrum clouds of routine. These pranks were always played upon those who were even less fortunate than they.

In almost every village there was a lad whose mental development had stopped at some stage of childhood. Such an unfortunate creature was the natural target of their attacks. These town simpletons were often tormented to a point of such desperation that they fled the village of their birth like hunted deer and were never seen again. Some cast themselves into rivers or deep wells to escape their pursuers.

This story is about such a Jewish village fool. It was told of a winter's evening by an old, bearded Jew in a crowded compartment of the train from Warsaw to Lodz. The listeners sensed that he had told the story many times before. There were no breaks in the narrative. Sometimes it seemed as though he were embellishing a point here and there as he went, but by the expression on his old face and the deep feeling in his voice, it was evident that the story had grown very close to his heart.

The small Jewish town from which the old man came—he was a teacher and cantor, like his fathers before him—had a young simpleton who was the envy of the entire region. He was the youngest son of a large family. To the great dissatisfaction of his parents he had entered this gloomy world late in their marriage. It was evident to them from the first that he lacked any physical beauty. The weak, scrawny body supported a head, much too large for it, covered with woolly red hair. His ears stuck out at an awkward angle. His features were irregular and his skin was wrinkled. His mouth was much too large and was shaped like that of a fish. Only in his large black eyes was there life—a dark, fearful spark of life. The rest of his face might have been the mask of an African tribe.

The fact that the child did not speak did not disturb the parents—for they had other children who had begun to speak quite late. But when finally, at an age when other children were already in school, the first sounds came from that fishlike mouth, they were forced to admit that the helpless babble would never develop into the wondrous music of human speech.

Abraham, for so they had named him, grew as it were in the dark, beneath the pitying eye of adults and the cruel derision of the young people. His walk was as clumsy as his speech. It was more like a swimming in air—his long arms thrust about in unison with his short, crooked legs. Even his own parents had to admit that these great, awkward movements of their son had a comic effect. The most sympathetic and well-meaning people could not restrain their laughter when they met Abraham on the street. But the boy paid no attention to other people. It did not make him unhappy that they laughed or mocked him wherever he went.

His father was a small alterations tailor, bent over his worktable from early morning into the night, when the dull light of two old-fashioned oil lamps illumined his work. His two eldest sons served as his helpers. The oldest daughter assisted her mother about the house, while the younger girls went to school. Abraham was not completely useless in the meager household. By the time he was ten he was trained to do the daily shopping. He gave the storekeeper his mother's list. Then he lugged his purchases home in a gray sack that hung heavy from his weak shoulders.

But the moment Abraham stepped into the street with his full sack every door opened and he was surrounded by a crowd of laughing and howling youngsters. The noise made him flinch briefly. Then he waddled in long, swimming motions toward his goal. Like marching soldiers the boys and girls fell in line behind him, imitated his step, and copied the sweeping motion of his arms. The few travelers who came to the town and stayed at the inn in the market place stopped in surprise when the strange procession passed them. But Abraham, after his initial fright, was more happy than otherwise to attract so much attention. It seemed to him that he marched at the head of a great army, a general who could count on the unconditional loyalty of his soldiers. The inhabitants of the town became accustomed to the sight and finally paid no attention to the noisy troupe. When they heard the laughter and hooting of the children in the street they only said, "There comes Red Abraham with his army!"

It was a bitter disappointment to the parents that this son would never learn to read and write like all the other children in the town in order to study the holy scriptures. The hardest burden for his father was the knowledge that Abraham would never undergo the sacred ceremony of Bar Mitzvah, would never be welcomed into the congregation as a full participant in the rites and the faith of Israel. Abraham's lips would never speak the benedictions over the Torah; he would never learn to pray to the God of his fathers.

When he took Abraham along to the house of study, where pious men argued over the interpretation of the Bible according to their ancient tradition, the boy lay at his feet like a poor little dog with its master and paid no attention to what was passing in the dusky chamber. Only when a miraculous story from the Bible was read aloud, he lifted his head for a moment to listen. It seemed at such times as though the thick fog that lay about his low forehead had lifted for a short while and a heavenly light were streaming into his dark existence. When the conversation was about angels and their messages of salvation, his misshapen mouth sometimes opened as though in anticipation of sweet nourishment. These brief glimmers of intelligence were strange and puzzling to all who witnessed them. To his parents they represented a slender hope that their child might some day improve. The honored rabbi, Samuel ben Isaac, whom the town revered as a saint, spoke words of hope to the father. "Unknown are the paths of the Lord," he said, "blessed be His holy name. What can we men know of His ways? Children and fools are often closer to His heart than the great and mighty of the earth. Read the sacred stories of the Bible to your child as often as possible. Only God knows how much he will understand."

One thing was certain: the boy knew his name. Whenever a voice spoke the name of Abraham, he turned to the speaker and his dull eyes came to life and acquired surprising depth. When the name of Abraham, the father of Israel, was spoken in the synagogue, he lifted his head toward the altar where his name had been pronounced.

One evening the Talmudists were arguing once again over the interpretation of the story of the sacrifice of Isaac. Abraham's father was an especially heated participant in the debate. Excitedly his bony finger, roughened by many needlepricks, underlined a passage in the Talmud that seemed to him the only acceptable interpretation of the dramatic anecdote of the struggle between fatherly love and love of God. Loud disputes and dark whispers flew this way and that among the bowed, bearded heads. Suddenly Abraham, who had been crouching on the floor, rose and stepped into the light of the dull lamp suspended from the low ceiling of the study. He stretched his long arms toward the light and twice burbled his name. "Abraham, Abraham." A strange, peaceful beatitude transformed his formless features as he spoke. Then the boy sank back into himself, his face lost all expression, and his wretched body fell again at his father's feet.

His father was filled with a great fear. Uncertainly he looked into the faces of his friends. The discussion was interrupted for some minutes and at last the rabbi decided to end it altogether for that evening. No one was able to say anything at all about this strange incident. But one thing was clear: the rough voice of the sick boy had been trying to proclaim a message. On their way home the men did not speak of the incident, but hastened their steps through the ill-lighted streets to their dark houses.

Now the tailor gave his wife a detailed, often exaggerated account of the singular happening. He became excited when she refused to attribute any deeper meaning to the incident. She reminded him of similar things that had happened with Abraham that had turned out to have no special import. The pale, thin wife of the tailor, aged prematurely through ten pregnancies, had not the slightest hope for her youngest offspring. Often she said with tears in her voice that it would be best for Abraham if God would take him soon. The sad stroking of her wilted hands over the flaming red hair of the child was her only expression of motherly feeling.

Of all the inhabitants of the town Abraham feared the blacksmith the most. He was more cruel to him than even the children. He inflicted on the child no mere practical jokes but a genuine inbred cruelty.

The blacksmith had enormous strength, a gigantic body, and a long black beard that hung over his bare, hairy chest. Everybody called him Goliath. His appearance did indeed bear a resemblance to the hair of that other giant, as described in the Bible. But there was no David in the town who dared to start a fight with this brute.

Goliath was proud of his strong muscles and felt that they made him superior to other people. Everyone admired him and was careful never to quarrel with him. The girls often gave him languishing glances, and it was no secret that several of them had fallen victim to his enticements. The blacksmith had a low opinion of scholarship and religion. Only on the very holiest days was he seen in the synagogue, wearing reasonably presentable clothes.

Goliath was the leader in all the pranks of the young people against the unhappy Abraham. He had appointed him the official town fool, and succeeded in having this honor conferred on the poor boy in a solemn ceremony. Trembling with fear, Abraham was dragged by the children to a field on the outskirts of town where

Goliath, surrounded by a stately assemblage, awaited him. Despairing and powerless, the tailor and his wife watched the ugly proceedings. The children danced a wild dance about the frightened boy, who was finally himself caught up in the mad commotion. A cringing smile appeared on his fish-mouth. With motions like the clumsy waddling of a duck he tried to join the circle of children, but each time they pushed him back into the center.

Then Goliath lifted his deep voice and called with exaggerated solemnity, "Abraham! Abraham!"

The boy rose and stepped before the smith as though driven by supernatural powers. Complete silence had fallen on the circle of children. It seemed as though the joke were to reveal a more serious significance. Again, this time in a portentous whisper, Goliath called, "Abraham! Abraham!"

The boy's red shock of hair sank humbly. He did not know what to expect from the strange call. His arms had ceased trembling. A deep silence was on all faces. Then a tall, thin girl stepped forward and, laughing loudly, set a brightly painted dunce cap on Abraham's head. But the intended cheering of the youngsters did not materialize. All eyes were fixed on the crowned king of fools, but Abraham stood with motionless features, sunk in stupor or in unknown dreams.

And thus it happened that the little meeting broke up more quickly than had been planned. Everyone had the feeling that the joke had misfired and that Goliath had suffered a defeat. Abraham was surprised to be left alone, and willingly followed some good-natured children from his neighborhood who took him home.

Time seemed to stand still in the boy's life. The fifteen-year-old was exactly like the ten-year-old. When he was twenty, his body had grown only a little and he appeared like a dwarf beside other young men of his age. Nor had his mental powers advanced at all. The others had taken their places in the active life of the town—Abraham remained the poor, useless child, good for nothing except his simple errands. He delivered the finished work from his father's tailor shop and sometimes got little presents from the customers, which he always gave to his mother. Sometimes the neighbors gave him errands to do and paid him with a few coins, for which he thanked them wordlessly with a quiet little smile.

Early on a summer's morning, while half the town was still asleep, Goliath appeared in the tailor's shop, to the great consternation of the family. Condescendingly he explained that he could use Abraham as an errand boy, too, and that he was prepared to pay the tailor well for his services. The parents divined an evil purpose behind these friendly words. They stood helplessly before the powerful man, at a loss what to do or say. They would have liked to turn him down, but that would only have meant more cruel pranks at Abraham's expense by the angry blacksmith. On the other hand, if they agreed, their son would be completely in the brute's power.

During this visit Abraham crouched on the floor as he had done since early childhood. He guessed nothing of the dark plans his dangerous enemy had brought. But in a few days' time he noticed that a great danger threatened his father's house. There was no laughter in the stuffy rooms, and his father stroked his hair with his workworn hands much more often than he had ever done. His mother kept glancing round and pressing him to her breast as though to protect him from invisible foes.

There was fear in the house of the tailor. It ate into the cracks of the dark walls, darkened the faces, and disturbed the sleep of parents and children. Abraham was seized by this fear without knowing its cause. But somehow he sensed that the hour of the great calamity was close at hand. He stared at the door as though the dark hour were about to cross the threshold.

That hour arrived on a bright Sabbath morning. Goliath appeared in his work-a-day clothes and said to the tailor and his wife, "Starting today I'm hiring Abraham."

He laid some money on the table as an advance on the wages. Then he turned to Abraham, stroked his face with his sooty paw in an unctuous show of friendship, and said, "Let's go, my boy."

But Abraham did not go without a struggle. He clung to the door jambs with his long fingers and screamed and howled like a whipped dog. His parents and brothers stood by helplessly. What could they do, what should they do? No one in the town could have advised them—they all feared the brute strength and cunning of the giant. So the old tailor and his wife spoke soothingly to their son. His mother quieted him with the sound of her voice.

"Abraham will come back to mother soon," she said. The tailor's wife spoke to her twenty-year-old son as she had done to the three-year-old of yore. "Abraham is just going to deliver some packages. He'll get lovely money for it, and then he can bring it to mother."

She always spoke very slowly to him, for the lad could understand only simple words and short phrases at a time. His consciousness accepted communications like a fluid, in small mouthfuls. Finally he stopped struggling, took Goliath's hand, and left his father's house with slow, waddling steps.

In the street the sight of the bearded giant leading the waddling dwarf attracted many people to their doorways. Goliath accompanied his victim with funny and exaggerated gestures. As always, many children followed Abraham up the street and formed a grotesque parade behind the pair. The news that Goliath was taking Abraham to his shop soon spread through the town. Laughter and sympathy surrounded the sad procession. As in his childhood, Abraham felt once again that he was the center of interest, and that calmed his fear a little. But he could not forget who was walking beside him this time, holding his fingers in a hard fist.

For the first few days everything went rather well. Abraham fulfilled his small duties with quiet industry. Sometimes he even smiled when the blacksmith made fun of his clumsy movements. Goliath had him deliver small tools he had repaired to the neighbors or perhaps a bill or two. Abraham generally knew the people to whom he had to take these things. The blacksmith pointed out the house with his finger. Often the little errand boy was treated to sweets or a piece of fruit. Those were happy moments for him. Surely they awakened in him a feeling of self-respect. Abraham never kept these small gifts. He always placed them in his mother's hands when he came home tired in the evening.

But soon the days grew dark in the blacksmith's shop. Goliath was following a diabolic plan that he had hatched a long time ago. He meant to increase the workload of his slave by degrees, at the same time making him more and more dependent upon him, and thus create situations that would serve for the general amusement, heighten his own fame, and satisfy his lust for power. Now they'd all see what a powerful, strong man the smith really was. That his physical strength surpassed that of anyone in town was an acknowledged fact—but this was not enough for him. He wanted to be followed everywhere by admiring glances. He wanted to be every young boy's hero and, above all, attract those smiles of young girls that promised the fulfillment of his desires.

It may seem strange that Abraham, of all people, was selected as the tool for such a purpose. But Goliath knew quite well what an important part the poor half-wit could play in his bid for power. First of all he was able to boast that he had a servant who must do for him what anyone else would certainly have refused to do. Even more important was the fact that the ridiculous aspect of the servant enhanced the popularity of the master by contrast.

Their walk to the blacksmith's shop on that very first day, and the laughter that followed the pair, were a matchless success for the blacksmith. For generations the townspeople would talk of that sight. The only photographer in town had stood on a street corner to take their picture.

After a few weeks the smith began to increase the loads Abraham had to carry. For he had noticed that physical exertion would disfigure the lad's features even more. His joy was boundless whenever he watched Abraham waddle over the uneven cobblestones carrying heavy wagonwheels that kept slipping from his clumsy fingers. His laughter roared and echoed from doors and windows like thunder. Often Abraham fell with the wheels, and then heavy tears fell from his despairing eyes. If a helpful hand was offered him, Goliath leaped to push it away. That was his answer to any show of humanity.

Thus the autumn approached. Every home was busy with preparations for the High Holy Days. Dedication and piety filled the hearts of the children. They remembered that it is part of the observance of these holiest of days that men practice love toward one another. The great day of confession and atonement was approaching. Young and old were anxious to purify their souls. Many of the children were ashamed of their treatment of Abraham and realized that it had been sinful. They vowed silently that they would never again be so heartlessly cruel.

Goliath noticed this change which threatened all his plans. He knew what was at stake. If the whole town turned against him, his hopes for fame would be dashed forever.

Something had to happen to improve his situation. He had misused Abraham for his ambitious purposes—but now he saw in him the originator of his misfortune and regarded him with hatred. He made the lad suffer more than ever.

Then suddenly the boy's luck seemed to turn. On the last Friday night before the New Year, long after services in the synagogues were over and the Sabbath candles in the homes of the town had burned to glimmering stubs, there was a knock at the door of the smithy and Goliath found on his threshold the only man in town in whose presence he felt, if not fear, at least a certain awe and uneasiness. It was the old rabbi. It was not his spiritual greatness that impressed Goliath, for that only made him laugh derisively, but there was a magic spell that emanated from the tall, grave figure. The rabbi's reputation as a holy man was based on his powerful glance almost more than on his great wisdom. Quiet and strength surrounded him when he read the Holy Scriptures in the synagogue or raised his dark voice to God. No one else possessed such power. His house was always full of people seeking advice, for he was able to offer assistance even in the most difficult situations of life. For the sick he always had a remedy in which they had more faith than in the medicines of the best physicians. In the most complicated matters of law he always knew the right answer.

The rabbi had come to see Goliath because Abraham's father had asked him to. He seemed to be the only one who might deliver his youngest son from the devilish hands of the blacksmith. The parents had witnessed diabolic dances that the black devil forced Abraham to do with him in the middle of the street. They sensed that worse torture was yet to come: the sad lips of their son were locked on the worst news.

The rabbi had listened to the tearful report of the parents, and had been silent for a long time. His fingers moved thoughtfully through his white beard.

Then he said, "Even Satan was once an angel of God. Nothing happens without the will of the Lord, blessed be His name. But a bad man must not trample the crop of the Lord."

They had expected advice, but he gave them none. They sensed, however, that he would travel the difficult road to the smithy.

Now he stood before the blacksmith. Through the door the light of the night sky poured into the obscure workshop. A reflection of the light was in the face of the old man. Searchingly he regarded the smith without a word.

"It is Sabbath Eve," he said then, "and you are still at work?"

He hardly expected an answer, and he got none.

Then the rabbi spoke of Israel, of the sorrows and sacrifices that the people had borne for centuries. He spoke of the trade of the smith, who fashions tools for the peaceful use of all people.

"Other peoples forge weapons with which to kill one another. They believe in their own might, but deep down they are the poorest of all. We are wounded by them, but we do not do battle, but bear our fate in humility. For peace is the will of God our Lord."

It seemed as though the old rabbi had forgotten the purpose of his visit. He spoke of many pious things, of the miracle of creation, the sanctity of the Sabbath, the chosen people, but not of the bad deeds of the smith. At times the blacksmith wanted to interject an impatient word into the speech of the old man, but he could not do it. The soft voice of the rabbi fell as heavily as the great hammer on the anvil.

Abraham's name was not mentioned. And why indeed? If the words of the pious man had found their way to the hardened heart, there would be no need of direct hints. And if it was impossible to change the ways of the blacksmith, then no power on earth could better Abraham's lot.

On the evening of the rabbi's visit Goliath's cronies waited in vain for him at the inn. They had been anticipating new plans and wild stories. When the evening passed quietly, they went home bored.

It was the eve of the New Year. Over the wide plain the sky still spread in deepest blue of summer. The flaming leaves were the only reminder of fall. A solemn peace came to every Jewish town of the district. Shops and stores closed early. The men attired themselves for the services, the women prepared the festival meal and covered the tables with fresh white cloths. Every face expressed pious solemnity.

On this day Abraham did not go to the blacksmith's but stayed at home. He had only one holiday coat to deliver for his father. The few people he met on the way were bound for the synagogue, an ungainly wooden building in a large square in the center of town. Like a heavy hand its high roof pressed on the low walls.

Abraham blundered through the deserted streets in his accustomed unsteady walk. Often he stopped and looked over his shoulder, expecting enemies on every hand. But the peace of the Holy Day seemed to extend even to Goliath and the children.

Suddenly he heard a high, ghostly voice calling through a side street, "Abraham! Abraham!"

He stopped, and looked in every direction. He even searched the ground and the trees, but there was no one. He continued on his way, slowly and more carefully than before. In his breast was the old fear. At the next street corner the same voice called his name, this time louder than before. Again Abraham searched in vain.

He could not dream that the one who called was running ahead of the poor town idiot up the next street, and hiding behind a door or tree until he reached the spot. Nor did he guess that the inventor of this joke, the son of the innkeeper, wanted less to frighten than simply to astonish him. Certainly he could not know that the visit of the rabbi had silenced his most formidable enemy.

It was all a horrible mystery to Abraham. In the hour of prayer he had been called by an invisible force. He was deeply moved. What did that solemn voice expect, so particularly of him? The poor little soul could not cope with that question. An unendurable pressure settled on his breast and spread to his brain, paralyzing his limbs. It was not fear or fright, but only an immense wonder that cast its spell over him. A high power had spoken to him and fastened him to the spot and to this moment, so that he could not move. Tears had welled up in his dark eyes. The long arms hung down the sides of the twisted body. Thus Abraham stood in the silence of the evening. In several windows the candles of the Holy Day glowed.

Suddenly a feeble memory awoke in Abraham's mind. A dusky evening in the house of study appeared before him, and he lay at his father's feet listening to the rabbi's words about the call of Abraham by the angels. And in the midst of this memory there came again, and this time nearer and more clearly, the call, "Abraham! Abraham!"

In that moment the spell released him and as though reacting to strong medicine life returned to the body of the idiot. For the first time his eyes gleamed with an intimation of joy. His hands felt along his body as though to ascertain that he was really there. Then his feet began to move again. The joyful smile remained on his features.

Just as lightning may momentarily illumine a black landscape, it had suddenly become clear to Abraham why he had had to suffer so much sorrow and distress through all his life. He had stepped into the light and had grasped the meaning of his sufferings. Out of the darkness of his youth he would now enter into the brilliance and glory of God. He believed it firmly.

At first Abraham's steps faltered along the empty streets. Then they became swifter and finally he began to run. Like a misshapen machine his body pushed forward. His arms and legs whirled like wheels about his body. His fish-mouth pushed whistling breaths into the night air like steam out of an overheated kettle.

The last light of day sank on the steep roof of the synagogue. As if drawn by a magnet Abraham moved toward that goal. His heart pounded as though it would burst the walls of his body. Gradually his strength began to fail and his steps became slower. At the end of his road the whirling and stamping of his limbs had dwindled away and he dragged his feet wearily.

Through the windows of the synagogue came the gleam of many

candles and the murmur of praying voices. Never before had Abraham's soul been stirred by these sounds; now they covered him like a warm garment.

Before the gutted door of the synagogue he stopped and tried to draw a deep breath. But only shrill whistling came from his breast. His arms clung to the doorpost. The large head sank to his chest and he trembled violently.

He stayed like that for several minutes. Then he began to relax. With great effort Abraham was able to open the door. With heavy feet he stepped into the large room that was filled with light and singing. The rasping of his breath drew the attention of several worshipers.

Abraham's eyes stared straight ahead in the direction of the Ark, where the cantor stood in his white prayer cloak. When his legs gave out, he crawled like an animal up the steps. His fingers grasped the gold-embroidered heavy curtain and tugged as though to pull it down. Then Abraham's voice screeched like the voice of a bird of prey. The congregation was frozen into horrified silence. All prayer had ceased and many books fell to the floor from trembling hands.

Again his voice was raised. It was like the voice of a little child, painstakingly putting together sounds that no one understands. It fought and begged for understanding. Finally it shaped words that everyone who stood near him could make out.

"Here am I!"

After this exertion his voice failed and turned into a faint choking sound. Abraham had dropped to the floor. Above him bent the benign face of the rabbi.

The rabbi saw the light fail in eyes that held a great secret. No one dared to speak until the silver beard was raised again. The rabbi's face was serious and deeply moved.

"Amen," said the rabbi, and the congregation repeated the holy word.

On the next day the blacksmith disappeared forever from the town.

(translated by Heni Wenkart)

David Plays Before Saul

(David spielt vor Saul)
After Rembrandt's painting

A shepherd boy, I play upon my lyre
before the ailing Saul, my noble king.
To him, whom God with wisdom did inspire,
my lips are bringing forth the psalms I sing.

Deep down into his soul my songs I'm sending
like buckets to the darkness of a well.
I saw a trembling crown through tears descending
on brows on which an anguished shadow fell.

More harsh than hunger pangs in hovels dreary
is my exalted ruler's great distress.
My tunes reflect his moans so low and weary,
the crimson curtain his unhappiness.

My prayerful songs shall follow Saul out yonder
to lands to which in dreams his mind will fly,
and on the carpet of my strains shall wander
his sorrow to the throne of God on high.

(translated by Karl F. Ross)

PART II
Literary Essays

Lessing and Judaism

I

His was the greatest and the most admirable character in German intellectual history. His mission has not come to an end but is particularly great in our time. "We need a man like Lessing," exclaimed Goethe. "For what makes him great is his character, his steadfastness. There are many people who are as intelligent and as educated, but where is there such a character?" His nature found expression in his life as well as his work. His life was struggle and humility, purity and want, humanitarianism and pain. He always remained poor and did not achieve great fame in his lifetime, but he never abandoned any of his convictions, and these convictions were the noblest possession of his century: a belief in the free human spirit, the duty to recognize all religions and nations, and the fight against poisoning of the spirit and bondage in the service of humaneness and progress.

Thus he is a leading figure in the eighteenth century that had such an abundance of great men and great ideas, an incomparable moral example. His poetic works and critical writings are imbued with this spirit of genuine and creative humanitarianism. The more proudly this spirit is manifested in them, the greater they are. This humanism is the inner fire in Lessing's works. It raises them above their purely artistic rank and makes them testimonials of a great creative character. The education of the human race—one would like to write this title of his moral testament over his entire work as well as the story of his life. He accomplished both with the greatest integrity.

His valor and the courage with which he took a stand made him lonely and knowing. He himself declared: "I am truly only a mill and not a giant. Here I stand in my place on a sand-hill outside the village. I come to no one and help no one, and I let no one help me." This is how proud he was of his independence and intellectual freedom. And yet he was a spokesman for his age, which is usually called the Age of Enlightenment and which stood for the rule of reason in all areas of life to the point of one-sidedness and exaggeration. In religion a "Christianity of reason" prevailed; it was averse to all orthodoxy and mysticism and rejected any dogmatism. But the most important thing about this conception of religion (which, incidentally, was greatly influenced by Spinoza) is the idea of tolerance. Lessing was the great exponent of this idea, and its greatest document is his drama *Nathan the Wise*. It is not accidental that a Jew is at the center of this classical German drama.

II

The entire Age of Enlightenment was of great significance for Jewry. Its tendencies toward tolerance, humanity, and reason were close to Judaism and, above all, of practical importance for the life of the Jews. Thus the spirit of the Enlightenment was decisive for the emancipation of the Jews; it opened to them the world of European culture and the road to social liberation. It is significant that the Jewish philosopher Moses Mendelssohn was one of the leaders of the Berlin Enlightenment; at the same time he was one of the closest personal friends of Lessing, who admired him equally for his intellect and his character. Lessing memorialized Mendelssohn in the figure of Nathan, and this figure in turn greatly contributed to decreasing scorn for the Jews in German society. Mendelssohn himself still was without civil rights. He received the right to reside in Berlin only as the bookkeeper of a factory. Suddenly he was an esteemed German man of letters, and people began to view the Jews from a different angle. A book like Christian Wilhelm Dohm's *Über die bürgerliche Verbesserung der Juden* [On the Civil Improvement of the Jews, 1781] proved to many that the decline of the Jews was due primarily to their lack of civil rights and their social position. Closer relations between Jews and Christians in the upper strata of the Berlin citizenry were in the offing.

Lessing had already defended Mendelssohn's co-religionists in a youthful work, the comedy *Die Juden* [The Jews, 1749, printed 1754]. "An excellent vindication of a despised people"—this is what a contemporary critic called the little play, whose literary importance is not very great. Lessing himself said about it: "It was the result of very serious reflection about the shameful suppression in which a people has to languish that, I should think, a Christian cannot regard without a kind of reverence. This people, I thought, once gave birth to so many heroes and prophets, and now people doubt whether an honest man may be found in its midst?" In the play a Jewish traveler saves a Christian estate owner from the clutches of robbers. When the Christian wants to express his appreciation to his rescuer, he receives this typically Lessingian response: "By way of recompense I ask only that in future you have a somewhat more gentle and less general judgment of my people. I did not hide from you because I am ashamed of my religion. But I noticed that you liked *me* and disliked my nation. The friendship of a human being, no matter who he may be, has always been of inestimable value to me." The more Lessing became the leader of the Enlightenment—at the same time far transcending it—the more he became a passionate proponent of the idea of tolerance and thus a defender of the Jews. He opposed the presumptuousness of every persuasion and fought not only religious intolerance but nationalism as well. Unlike Leibniz, he did not believe that we are living in the best of all possible worlds: "Is God to have part in everything except our mistakes?"

Among Lessing's Berlin acquaintances was the physician Aaron Salomon Gumpertz, a man profoundly versed in philosophy and literature. Through him Lessing met "Herr Moses" in 1754, and shortly thereafter he described him in a letter as follows: "He really is a Jew. . . . From the outset I regard him as a credit to his nation, provided his own co-religionists, who have always been impelled by an unfortunate spirit of persecution against people of his kind, allow him to mature. His integrity and his philosophical mind already lead me to regard him as a second Spinoza, who lacks nothing but his mistakes to be completely equal to him."

Lessing overestimated Mendelssohn's importance as a philosopher and writer. Mendelssohn's best work is in the field of psychological aesthetics. But Lessing recognized something else in him: an intellectual friend of moral nobility with whom he could engage in intelligent and profound conversations. Mendelssohn's philosophical training was better than Lessing's. Without him Lessing's main work in the philosophy of art, *Laokoon*, might never have been written. Their lively correspondence enhanced their friendship, which also produced a joint work, *Pope a Metaphysician!*

The literary apotheosis of Lessing's humanism and his friendship with Mendelssohn came in *Nathan the Wise*, a drama that belongs to world literature. Didactically, perhaps too much so, and yet poetically and in a humanly moving way, Lessing proclaims his message: "Let each one strive to show a love that is uncorrupted and free from prejudice." If Shakespeare's Jew Shylock is the representative of the principle of hate, Lessing's Nathan embodies the principle of love for one's fellow man. In no other character in German literature have philanthropy and toleration, equality of rights and lack of prejudice found such beautiful and kindly expression. The play's effect was a new attitude toward the Jews among the educated society of Germany. People spoke of the Jews as the people of Nathan and Mendelssohn.

The *raison d'être* of all religions is shown by means of the famous Ring Parable. It is an ancient Jewish heritage, probably going back to a Spanish Jew around the year 1100. Rabbi Salomo ben Verga then gave it its first compact form in his *Shebet Yehuda*. The parable traveled through all literatures and assumed its classic form in

Boccaccio's *Decameron*. This is how it reached Lessing. It is at the center of a work that honors the ideal of humanity as well as Judaism. The new and unique feature is that a Jew is presented as a human ideal. Sultan Saladin speaks these beautiful words: "I have never demanded that all trees should have the same bark." But Nathan is a tree of a very special kind, which makes the Templar exclaim rapturously: "What a Jew! And one who wants to be taken only for a Jew." Therefore, to be truly a human being it is important to be true and genuine. This is Nathan's whole secret, and it is the secret of every humanistic *Weltanschauung*. In *Nathan the Wise* this *Weltanschauung* has become a religion, the religion of modern man. Lessing proclaims it as its greatest and purest priest. After Lessing's death Mendelssohn summed up the fame of this work and its moral effect upon his contemporaries in these words: "He wrote *Nathan the Wise* and died." No greater peak was imaginable.

III

The Nathan religion is effective in some of Lessing's theoretical writings as well, notably in his moral testament, *The Education of the Human Race*. In this work a kind of religious philosophy of history is developed. Lessing declares that God trained his initially crude people of Israel to be the educators of the human race. "But, it will be asked, why train such a crude people, with which God had to start from scratch? I reply: In order that in the course of time He might all the better employ particular members of this nation as the educators of all other peoples. He was bringing up in them the future educators of the human race. These were Jews, these could only be Jews, only men from a nation that had been educated in this way."

With these words Lessing once more made the Jews the bearers of his humanism and educators of the human race, as he had done in *Nathan the Wise*. There is no grander view of the Jewish spirit than this one, nor is there a mission that is as hard and as painful. We must never forget this. This is the ultimate demand that Lessing made of Jewish posterity.

(translated by Harry Zohn)

Bettina von Arnim
and the Jews

> My great talent is loving.
> —Bettina

I

Bettina von Arnim did not have the penetrating intelligence of Rahel Varnhagen nor the epic talent of Dorothea Schlegel nor the power of fascination of Caroline Schlegel, the wife of August Wilhelm von Schlegel, poet and translator of Shakespeare. Neither did she possess the poetic gift of her unfortunate friend, Karoline von Günderode.[1] But though she was not the greatest woman of German Romanticism, she was certainly the most brilliant.

Just as all these women were very different from one another, so the Romantic movement was by no means uniform and followed no fixed pattern. Its character can really be determined only negatively, through its fight against rationalism and classicism and against every restriction on the freedom of the individual. In this movement, for the first time in German intellectual history, Jews took an active part, especially Jewish women. The salons of Berlin Jewesses were the meeting places of writers, artists, and scholars. The great

Protestant theologian and philosopher Friedrich Schleiermacher, and even a member of the royal family, Prince Louis Ferdinand of Prussia, were frequent visitors there and carried on a lively correspondence with these Jewish patronesses of learning and the arts.

Rahel Varnhagen, née Levin (1771–1833), who was married to the diplomat and writer Karl August Varnhagen von Ense (1785–1858), called her salon "the mirror and the abbreviated chronicle" of her times.[2] Dorothea Schlegel (1764–1839), the oldest daughter of Moses Mendelssohn, was married to the leading critic of the Romantic movement, Friedrich von Schlegel (1772–1829). She was a close friend of Henriette Herz (1764–1847), the gifted wife of the physician-philosopher Markus Herz, one of the earliest champions of Kant's philosophy.

Bettina Brentano von Arnim (1785–1859) was the most human and most universal of all Romantic women. Her life and her work were the expression of her ever-enthusiastic, ever-active personality, one that was incomparable in its strength of feeling, unrestraint, and courage. Wilhelm von Humboldt wrote about young Bettina in 1808: "Such liveliness, such leaps of thought and head—for, one moment she sits on the floor, the next on the stove—so much foolishness is unheard of."[3] Especially impressive is the description that Caroline Schlegel gives in a letter of the same year to Pauline Gotter: "She is a wondrous little creature, a veritable Bettine [from Goethe's *Venetian Epigrams*] in physical pliancy and suppleness; inwardly sensible, but outwardly quite foolish; respectable and yet beyond all respectability; everything she is and does is not entirely natural, and yet it is impossible for her to be any different."[4] Thirty years later Jacob Grimm offered this evaluation: "She is an overflowing fountain who does not allow herself and others calm moderation of thought."[5]

As the sister of the poet Clemens Brentano and later as the wife of the poet Achim von Arnim, she was in the center of Late Romanticism. But she always remained open to life and its movements. In the era of Young Germany Heinrich Laube coined the expression "Bettina Boldness." Karl Gutzkow, in his autobiography, gives us a graphic picture of a visit to the aged Bettina and speaks of "two hours of conversation unforgettable to me." He calls her a "fluttering sylph" who is always ahead of a man's deliberate seriousness.[6]

In the face of all social conventions, and of religion as well, she preserved her individual freedom. She dreamed of a new world religion, but was impressed by Schleiermacher's Christianity of emotions. She was as free from religious prejudice as from the social and national arrogance all around her. In this she differed especially from her brother Clemens, seven years her senior, who kept admonishing his sister to lead a more settled life. But Bettina confessed: "My soul is a passionate dancer; it leaps about to an inner dance music which I can hear and others cannot."[7] When King Frederick William IV of Prussia planned to build a cathedral in Berlin,[8] she exclaimed: "Build it in those scattered huts in Silesia![9] A dome in which the God of humanity reigns, every fireplace a sacrificed altar of compassion, of love of mankind."[10]

From her earliest youth this ardent love of mankind attracted her to all needy creatures. Through her association with them she dared to defy her own social circle, which she found boring and despised. People wanted to educate her into an "agreeable and amiable girl," but that seemed not at all pleasant to her, indeed quite "horrible." About the rich citizens of Frankfurt she writes to horrified Clemens, whose "barbaric sister" she calls herself: "In the streets there is the smell of chaffering; on Sundays the shops are closed! What is there behind those iron bars and grates? Chaffering, money! What do people do with their money? Ah! They give banquets, they get dressed up and ride in back of the carriage with two servants. . . . All wealth is a stuffed figure which one can use for display, and the loafers are hungry horses; they don't care if the one of whom they eat their fill loses his bowels." The more Clemens exhorted Bettina to lead a conventional life, the more savagely she rebelled: "But morality and respectability, these are two stupid watchmen blocking the path of human existence and volition."

This youthful defiance drove Bettina out of the houses of the patricians and to the poor, the destitute, the residents of the suburbs and the *Judengasse*, the Frankfurt ghetto. They were all closer to her heart than her own class, which Clemens respected so highly. In deep seriousness she acknowledged: "I know what I need. I need to keep my freedom. Freedom for what? For accomplishing and completing what my inner voice directs me to do."

It was this inner voice that led her to an unprecedented provocation of the so-called "fine society" and to a free, untrammeled way of living. In her old age she went even beyond that and aligned herself with political rebellion and the fight on behalf of all oppressed people. Goethe considered children rigorists. Bettina became a rigorist at the end of her life.

II

When Bettina was born in Frankfurt in 1785, the character of the *Judengasse* was probably still the same as Goethe had found it as a boy and described it in his autobiography. Conditions there were among the "things full of presentiment which crowded in on the boy and probably on the youth as well." Although he was repelled by the narrowness, the squalor, the swarming, the inhabitants were to him "nevertheless the chosen people of God and, no matter how things had turned out, they walked about in memory of the oldest times."[11]

There is hardly any doubt that Bettina's descriptions of her visits to the Frankfurt ghetto[12] influenced Goethe's presentation, just as she had a large general share in the genesis of Goethe's autobiography *Fiction and Truth (Dichtung und Wahrheit)*. In her old age Bettina herself gave us a lively, colorful, and at the same time grim picture of the *Judengasse* in her work *Dies Buch gehört dem König* (1843).

In Bettina's youth it seemed as though the walls of the ghetto would crumble forever. After the Congress of Vienna (1815) and the ensuing reactionary epoch, however, the Frankfurt Senate sought to restore all former restrictions on the Jewish inhabitants. The struggle for the enforcement of equal civil rights went on for ten years, a struggle in which the Jews did not achieve complete success. It disturbed the social peace of the city, leading to anti-Jewish outbreaks on the part of the rabble. Only in 1824 was a kind of compromise between the Senate and the Jewish Community effected, but it complied primarily with the desires of the ruling class.[13]

In this struggle for power, which both sides also fought with pamphlets, Bettina's brother-in-law, Karl Friedrich von Savigny, the head of the "Historical School of Law," played a sorry role.[14] He had endorsed an opinion of the Faculty of Law at the University of Berlin that was intended to prove that the Frankfurt Jews had no claim to citizenship and that the ghetto had to continue.

Equality in civil rights for the Jews of Frankfurt, which had already been promulgated by the French general Jourdan, was confirmed by the ruler of the Grand Duchy of Frankfurt, Karl Theodor von Dalberg.[15] Dalberg was a rather ambiguous, opportunistic, insincere man. All of Bettina's statements about him indicate that she considered him malicious and disagreeable; he called Bettina "the little friend of the Hebrews." He was among the originators of the new municipal regulations of November 30, 1807, regarded by the Jews as a severe disappointment, and which provoked a polemical reply from Ludwig Börne.[16] In 1821 Börne wrote of the conditions in Frankfurt: "In Frankfurt, where I live, the word 'Jew' is the inseparable shadow of all occurrences, all relationships, of every pleasant and unpleasant matter." On the Jewish side, the religious reformer, philanthropist, and pedagogue, the Privy Financial Counselor Israel Jacobson (1768-1828), stood out as a leader.[17]

Bettina tried to interest Goethe in this Jewish struggle for rights, as can be seen from her book *Goethes Briefwechsel mit einem Kinde* (1835). She sent him various pamphlets and called his attention to the Jewish journal *Sulamith*, the organ of Israel Jacobson, published at Dessau from 1806 on, which stood for ideals of civilization and humanity. Its readership included many Christian intellectuals such as Dalberg and Bettina herself. On March 30, 1808, she wrote to Goethe about the journal: "I am enclosing everything that has appeared to date, except for a journal which the Jews publish under the title *Sulamith*. It is very prolix. If you want it, I shall send it to you, because the Jews present it to me as their protectress and little helper in need."[18]

Goethe greatly underestimated the extremely energetic and manifoldly talented Israel Jacobson, whose reforms of Jewish religious services aroused even the interest of the philosopher Schleiermacher. He mocked at the "Jewish Savior" *(Judenheiland)* of Brunswick without knowing much about him. But to Bettina, Jacobson was not only the most prominent opponent of Dalberg, but also a pedagogical reformer. He had founded, in 1801, a new type of educational institution at Seesen in the Harz Mountains, where Jewish and Christian boys and girls were to be introduced to German culture. It was the spirit of Enlightenment and Neo-Humanism that prevailed in this and other pedagogical experiments of that type, including the "Philanthropin" in Frankfurt. To Goethe Bettina confessed that she had little interest in these new schools, with the exception of the Philanthropin, which she often visited.

The faculty of the latter institution included Christian teachers. Among them was Joseph Franz Molitor (1779–1860), one of the most peculiar among the many eccentric figures of Late Romanticism.[19] In his youth Molitor had been influenced by his study of the writings of Kant, Fichte, and Schelling, later also of Franz von Baader, the Catholic theologian and philosopher who tended toward theosophy and mysticism. He had published books on the philosophy of civilization and of religion. When at the beginning of the century the Philanthropin opened its doors, Molitor joined this institute as a teacher as well as a pupil. He studied Hebrew, Aramaic, the Talmud, the Kabbalah, and the Zohar, in order to increase his knowledge of Judaism. These studies found a fruitful expression in his philosophical magnum opus, *Philosophie der Geschichte oder über die Tradition* (Philosophy of History or On Tradition), which appeared in four volumes between 1824 and 1853. The final volumes of this work attempt a systematic presentation of the Kabbalah, that intricate, many-layered, mysterious Jewish mysticism which had spread in several European countries since the thirteenth century. Molitor found the Kabbalah far superior to Christian mysticism in religious depth and poetic magic, and generally placed the original faith of the Jewish Bible far above that of the New Testament.

Molitor did much to shape Bettina's views on religion and history. Their conversations estranged both from Christianity and aroused in them a lively interest in Judaism. Bettina was so greatly impressed by Molitor that she could not talk enough about him. In her letters to Goethe and to her friend Karoline von Günderode she called him "my Molitor." He served as guide on her visits to the Philanthropin.

There were, however, in Frankfurt, still people like the historian Voigt who found it ridiculous that Molitor should examine Jewish children in Greek and Roman history. Bettina was outraged at this arrogance. She liked to visit the Jewish model school "because of the poor Jewish children who, together with the Christians, received their tiny little share of humane treatment there; and, if I may say so, this seemed to me an education in itself: to accustom children of the same age and the same ability from an early age to the fact that they have equal human rights, whether they be Jews or Christians."

It was entirely in this spirit that Molitor conceived of his pedagogical mission. Bettina tried to convince Goethe of the truth of these ideas: "This high-minded man believes that, since he has a body to sacrifice to the Jews and a mind to devote to them, both should be employed very usefully." At the same time she declined to speak to Dalberg again about the situation of the Jews, as Goethe wished her to do. That ruler saw only the vices and not the virtues of the Jews. "Their kind," said Bettina, "is, after all, humankind, and it ought to enjoy freedom for once." Thus she called Molitor's idea to get Christian and Jewish children into one school a happy one.

III

In the wide panorama that Bettina's second book of letters, *Die Günderode* (1840), offers us, there appears a touching marginal figure, Bettina's "Autumn Jew," old Ephraim from Marburg. Bettina succeeded in arousing a lively interest in him in her friend

Karoline von Günderode. The latter was also a woman free of prejudice and with humane feelings; otherwise no intimate friendship between the two Romantics could have developed. Bettina is very specific in describing her first meeting with old Ephraim, which took place in Marburg at the home of Professor Weiss: "The most handsome man! A white beard of half an ell, big brown eyes, a beautiful simple figure, the calmest forehead, a splendid, majestic nose, an orator's lips from which wisdom must resound sweetly." Everyone showed old Ephraim great reverence, although he was only a poor Jewish tradesman. He had once been a teacher of mathematics and had had students in Giessen and in Marburg, but had been obliged to make money and had thus become a dealer in clothing.

Rarely in her life did Bettina find such a kindly and wise conversational partner. Their talks were continued in Frankfurt, where Ephraim became a sort of private tutor to Bettina. He taught her mathematics and through his teaching rescued her from the "moth damage of domesticity." Bettina saw in him another Socrates; from him she learned to place the world of intellectual values above all other worlds and she asked him about everything that came to her mind.

Among other things, the two discussed the destiny of the Jews. Bettina instilled confidence in the old man: "At least you are closer to truth than others who consider a Jew an oppressed man; freedom rises from within, and a drop of it is enough to lift us above all scorn." Ephraim bitterly acknowledged: "It is the Jew's path to creep through the thorns and thistles with which the Christians block his way, and he must be fearful of waking the dogs that will pursue him through the thorns so that he can proceed neither forward nor backward and often perishes in the sweat of his toil, and, sadder still, no longer finds his God in his own heart."

To Bettina this simple old man was a great model "who fulfils the difficult conditions of his life beyond the declining bloom of his children, takes every laborious step toward the preservation of grandchildren, no longer spends any day as his own, does not pay any attention to himself, wandering to his family in the heat of day, stooping with an effort in order to gather the bread-crumbs on his path and to bring them to orphaned children." Bettina's language acquires an especial warmth and emotion when she tells about her visits with this old man whose life appears to her pure communication with the divine.

The story of Bettina's friendship with a young seamstress, Veilchen by name, reads like a tender novel. Veilchen was a little older than Bettina. An excellent embroiderer who lived in the ghetto, she taught this art to the wealthy families of the city. Bettina admired her skill; she had respect for every activity and consequently could not muster any pity for the French émigrés who mourned for their past life of leisure. This poor, humble, industrious girl bore her hard fate silently and serenely. Bettina's relationship with her transcended every social prejudice of her class. But never before had her actions aroused such wrath in her circle as did this harmless association. There is an account of it in Bettina's fourth book, *Clemens Brentanos Frühlingskranz* (Clemens Brentano's Spring Wreath), published in 1844, which presents the story of the brother's and sister's youth on the basis of their correspondence between 1800 and 1803, the fifteenth to the eighteenth years of Bettina's life.

Bettina's cordial friendship with the poor Jewish girl was a protest against the arrogance of the rich as well. Once she brought her the first violets she had found—an allusion to her name. Another time she came upon her friend while she was sweeping the staircase with a broom. "Oh, let me sweep a little, too," said Bettina and took the broom from her. This incident became known in the city. The scandal reached Clemens's ears, but Bettina could only laugh. She wrote her brother: "I just wanted to spin a little innocent thread in the web of the world, one tiny little thread, and—no, I am supposed to break it, because it is not the thing to do."

Bettina learned from Veilchen many Jewish religious customs, and was especially charmed by the celebration of *Rosh Chodesh* and the blessing of the moon *(Birkhath Levanah)*. "And a Jew laments and prays that the hatred of his enemies may not blind him and their scorn not crush him. He places himself before the judge's bench of the moon, and on his way home from alien places he opens his garment to the light of the new moon so that it may shine upon his chest. Even though this may be nothing but custom, still it indicates that he wants to be lifted up to a higher sphere by the New Moon; he asks the powers of Nature to lift him up. How beautiful this is and how much truer than if I make an index of my sins and beg God to cancel this bad balance sheet!"

Bettina wanted to bring German poetry to her young friend, and while Veilchen threaded her needles, she read to her poems of Goethe. To brotherly reproaches she paid no attention. It seemed to her as though she and her brother spoke different languages. Why should the gossip of "fine society" concern Bettina? Clemens knew his sister's obstinacy "in offering defiance when you consider something right."

The further course of this tender friendship is not known to us. Presumably it waned when Bettina left Frankfurt. To Bettina it meant, among other things, the justification of her faith and her character: "You forbid me to associate with a poor Jewish girl; and I want to associate with everything that lives in this world as my contemporary."

IV

The aging Bettina was a dauntless fighter. Social sentiments, love of mankind, the libertarian urge of her youth—these had now become political demands for which she fought courageously and passionately. During the Berlin cholera epidemic in 1831 she fearlessly visited the sick, who venerated her as their angel, and supplied them with food and medicine. When, in 1837, seven liberal professors of the University of Göttingen were removed from their posts, she aroused the public and succeeded in securing for Jacob and Wilhelm Grimm, the masters of German philology, a call to Berlin. She used her personal connection with King Frederick William IV, whom she knew as crown prince, to obtain a pardon for the revolutionary writer Gottfried Kinkel. In her correspondence with the king and in connection with the sentencing of Gottfried Kinkel, she expressed her hope for complete religious tolerance in Prussia. On July 29, 1849, she wrote: "The most praiseworthy thing in the Prussian land, especially under Your Majesty's government, is the complete religious tolerance."[20]

In the field of religion she drew farther and farther away from the doctrines of the Church, in marked contrast with her brother Clemens, who thought he could find peace of soul in making a Catholic cross. She hoped for a social kingdom from Frederick William IV. How bitter was her disappointment!

Bettina's work *This Book Belongs to the King* (1843) is one of the most significant manifestoes of the political, social, and religious fight for freedom of this revolutionary decade. Bettina sent the king a copy with a letter, but no answer is known to us. This late work has the same loose form as Bettina's youthful writings. It constitutes a mixture of personal documents, such as letters and conversations, and fictional episodes.

By this time her attitude toward public life had become much more radical. She now came out far more passionately than before for the rights of the Jews.[21] In the first volume there are only occasional passages on this subject, but the second, subtitled "Conversations with Daemons," contains a full expression of her political convictions. At the beginning there is the beautiful story, "The Convent Berry" *(Die Klosterbeere)*, with this dedication: "In memory of the *Judengasse* at Frankfurt." The dedication bears the date of Goethe's birthday, August 28, 1808. With her old passion for freedom Bettina even addresses herself to the nuns: "You, too, little nuns, who no longer turn and stir in your cells, dead to life, who no longer have any aim in life but to tell your beads with folded hands, if you break the shell, then you will fly into the sea of freedom again." These reflections lead her to the beautiful words: "Doubts are not errors and vows of faith are no crime against love; they transfigure the spirit and are shipwrecked on it which circumscribes the divine in the sea of creation and is submerged in it, casting off all garments in order to be free, naked, immaculate—and all searching is religion."

That is why Bettina wanted to be protectress of the suppressed in the spiritual field, too. In this connection her memories go back to the Frankfurt *Judengasse,* to the "brethren of Nathan the Wise," who dwelt in the narrow, dark houses, and to the children to whom she used to give flowers. Once more she conjures up the memory of the Primate von Dalberg who has been dead since 1817 but against whom she continues to bear a grudge. In an imaginary conversation Bettina has the ruler say bad things about the Jews, attributing to them the mind of usurers, filth, irresponsibility, egotism. In the face of such cheap accusations Bettina declares angrily: "A Christian makes an idol of superstition; it is his Christ." Her profound love of mankind transcended all dogmatic religions. She vigorously rejected attempts at converting the Jews.[22] To the Primate's question as to whether she does not consider Christianity to be truer than Judaism, she replies mockingly: "For a primate it is, but not for a rabbi." The idea that Christ was a Jew is at the center of this theological discussion. Thus she turned against a Church "which ejects the tribe of its founder from its bosom, an unmixed race equipped by Nature as one of its noblest, with keen senses and deep feelings." She recognized only one single religious commandment: "Love ye one another!" Her libertarian beliefs inevitably led Bettina to the idea of a religion of human conscience as the sole mediator between the human and the divine. In this faith she saw triumph over all existing religions.

In Bettina's lovingkindness toward Jews and Judaism we must recognize the expression of a personality burning for freedom and justice, a personality that drove her to the side of the political rebels. So she cried out to the Prussian king in the tempestuous year of 1848: "There is a free kindness and goodness, but also a gentleness and greatness of soul that arises from maturity of the mind, which atones for all guilt."

(translated by Harry Zohn)

NOTES

1. See Margarete Susman, *Frauen der Romantik* (Jena, 1929).
2. Bertha Badt, *Rahel und ihre Zeit* (Munich, 1912), p. 9.
3. Herbert Levin-Derwein, *Die Geschwister Brentano* (Berlin, 1927), p. 100.
4. Reinhard Buchwald, ed., *Carolinens Leben in Briefen* (Leipzig, 1923), p. 493.
5. Levin-Derwein, *Die Geschwister Brentano*, p. 158.
6. *Gutzkows Werke*, ed. Peter Müller (Leipzig, 1911), 3:113ff.
7. All quotations from Bettina's works are based on her *Sämtliche Werke*, ed. Waldemar Oehlke, 7 vols. (Berlin, 1922). The most recent books on Bettina are: Arthur Helps and Elizabeth Jane Howard, *Bettina* (New York, 1957), and Ina Seidel, *Drei Dichter der Romantik* (Stuttgart, 1956). See also the article by Bertha Badt, "Eine Judenfreundin in der deutschen Romantik," *Israelitisches Familienblatt*, No. 30 (1926), pp. 11 ff.
8. See H. S. Reiss, *Political Thought of the German Romantics* (Oxford, 1955).
9. A reference to the starving Silesian weavers; cf. Gerhart Hauptmann's drama *Die Weber*.
10. Letter to Wilhelm von Humboldt, dated June 22, 1844; Levin-Derwein, *Die Geschwister Brentano*, p. 138.
11. *Goethes Werke*, *Jubiläums-Ausgabe* 22: 175 f.
12. Compare the description by Achim von Arnim in his story, "Die Majoratsherren." L. Achim von Arnim, *Novellen*, ed. Rudolf Kayser (Munich, 1918), pp. 64 ff. The history of the Frankfurt ghetto is treated by L. Kracauer, *Die Geschichte der Judengasse in Frankfurt a.M.* (Frankfurt a.M., 1906).
13. On the Jews in Frankfurt and their persecution during the period of the Restoration, see A. Freimann and I. Kracauer, *Frankfort* (Philadelphia, 1929); Eleonore O. Sterling, "Anti-Jewish Riots in Germany in 1819," *Historia Judaica*, 12 (1950): 105 ff.; Heinz Bender, *Der Kampf um die Judenemanzipation in Deutschland im Spiegel der Flugschriften 1815-1820* (Jena, 1939); Siegfried Scheuermann, *Der Kampf der Frankfurter Juden um die Gleichberechtigung 1815-1824* (Kallmünz, 1933).
14. He was married to Kunigunde (Gunda) Brentano.
15. On Dalberg's attitude toward the Jews of Frankfurt, see Freimann and Kracauer, *Frankfort*, 193 ff. Dalberg was the oldest brother of the manager of the Mannheim theater, a friend of Friedrich Schiller's.
16. Börne's pamphlet is reprinted in his *Gesammelte Schriften*, vol. 2 (Hamburg, 1862-1863); also in Börne, *Über den Antisemitismus* (Vienna, 1885).
17. For bibliography on Jacobson, see *Encyclopaedia Judaica*, (1931), 8:745 f.
18. The text of Bettina's original letters to Goethe dealing with these pamphlets is almost identical with the letters as they appear in her first book, *Goethes Briefwechsel mit einem Kinde* (1835).
19. On Molitor, see *Jewish Encyclopaedia* (1904), 8:651.
20. Levin-Derwein, *Die Geschwister Brentano*, p. 158.
21. Moritz Carriére's view that only her friendship with young Heinrich Bernhard Oppenheim was responsible for this championship of his co-religionists must be rejected.
22. Schleiermacher, too, opposed all attempts to convert Jews; he looked upon such conversions as expressions of indifference toward either religion.

"Telling the News"
A Chapter of Thomas Mann's Novel
Joseph the Provider

I

When Goethe praised the loveliness of the biblical Joseph story, but stated with regret that it was so short that one was tempted "to depict it minutely,"[1] he scarcely knew that this wish had already been fulfilled, to a great extent, in the Middle Ages. From the second to the thirteenth century, the European Jews had created pious legends centered on biblical characters, and especially on Joseph, and told these stories again and again in every generation. In this world of fairy tales, enriched by the fertile imagination of biblical commentators, children grew up. In Hebrew, German-Jewish, and Spanish-Jewish anthologies these legends have been preserved for us.[2] Until the eighteenth century they had been kept alive by oral transmission. They had been known outside the walls of the Jewish quarters, too. Even the Fathers of the Church knew and loved these religious legends. When the oral transmission came to an end, scholars, of whom Israel Benjamin Levner (1862–1916) was the most distinguished, took care of these literary treasures. Levner was followed by L. Ginsberg, Micha Josef bin Gorion, and others.

The Joseph stories among these legends are so closely interrelated that they appear almost like a continuous novel.[3] The transitions between the different stages of this fabulous biography, only slightly touched upon in the Bible, are dealt with in much greater detail in these medieval tales.[4]

One of the most beautiful of the Joseph stories deals with Serach, the daughter of Asher who was the son of Jacob. The basis of the plot of the story is a psychological consideration as to how Jacob should be prepared for the great news that his favorite son Joseph, believed dead these many years, has been found to be alive. This question must have been considered by the Jewish theologians and Bible commentators of the Middle Ages of such great importance that they eventually invented the beautiful Serach legend, which was at the same time human and poetical.[5]

When Joseph's brothers were returning home from Egypt, bringing with them not only strange fruits and treasures but also a memory of the great experience of the meeting with their brother, they thought much of how to break the astonishing news of his being found alive to their old father. Joseph himself, fearing that the shock of the sudden news might endanger the life of the old man, had warned his brothers in the hour of their departure to prepare the ground for the news very slowly and carefully.

To this problem the legend offers a most convincing solution. When the brothers reentered the land of Canaan, they were greeted by the girl Serach, Asher's daughter. "She was a good and clever girl and knew how to play on the harp." She undertook to carry out the brothers' instructions to tell her grandfather through a song about how Joseph had been found again in Egypt. And over and over again, in her lovely, childlike voice, Serach sang this one sentence: "Joseph, my uncle, lives. He is ruler over all the land of Egypt." This song the patriarch Jacob enjoyed, much as if it were a beautiful dream. The spirit of the Lord seemed to rest upon him, and he blessed his granddaughter, wishing her that death might never claim her. Again and again he asked her to repeat the words that gave him much joy.

As a result, the patriarch was put in such high spirits that he was able to receive the great message without much shock. When the brothers arrived, they repeated the news that Joseph was alive and was the ruler of all Egypt. Jacob, however, could not yet accept the news of the miracle. He was convinced of its truth only when he saw Joseph's presents and heard in detail the story of the meeting and the mutual recognition. Then, with reawakened manly resoluteness, he expressed the wish to go to Egypt to his son in order to see him once again before his own death.

The legend describes further how Jacob, who since Joseph's disappearance had continuously mourned his son, came back to life. He distributed gifts, he had his hair cut, he put on the new Egyptian robes sent him by Joseph, and he invited the most eminent people of Canaan to a feast that lasted three days.

II

When Thomas Mann decided to include this medieval legend in his Joseph novel, he faced a double task: to adjust it to the narrative rhythm of his story and also to the philosophical character of his great work. Both necessities forced him to a far-reaching elaboration of the motifs and the happenings of the legend. Thus this chapter, "Telling the News,"[6] gives the impression of an independent tale in which miraculous events, psychological characterizations, and religious meanings are combined.

The preceding chapter, "How Shall We Tell Him?", belongs to the plot of the episode. Contrary to the old legend, Joseph, in Mann's novel, did not give any advice to his brothers in the farewell hour about how they were to inform their father of the great news. The problem originates during the seventeen-day journey home when many suggestions and possibilities are discussed by the brothers. "Children, you will see, we shall have him falling on his back when we tell him, unless we go about it very tactfully and cautiously. . . . The question is, how to tell him so that the joy shall not be too abrupt and we do not suddenly thwart his settled sorrow." How difficult also to persuade the old man to undertake the long trip to Egypt for the visit to which, in Mann's novel, not only Joseph, but

Pharaoh, too, had invited him! Oriental fatalism leads to the decision: "The hour will come, and the moment whisper us how we shall use it." A messenger would have to be sent to the father, first, to prepare him.

Thus, the meeting with the sweetly singing girl appears no longer as a pure accident, but almost as the gift of a higher providence. Serach is a tool of destiny, fated for an important mission. Thomas Mann, therefore, describes in detail her lovely bearing so that she might be recognizable as a worthy instrument for her task. She is shown at first in the framework of a rich spring landscape, sitting on a rock, her zither in her hands. She herself is like a flower: "It was a little maid, alone under the wide sky, in a red smock, with daisies in her hair." She is twelve years old, on the threshold of womanhood. All her feelings and emotions are expressed in her music. Dan, her clever uncle, rather than Asher, her father, acts as spokesman for the returning brothers, and asks Serach to sing to her grandfather a song telling the good news of Joseph's rescue and present whereabouts. She accepts this offer intelligently and readily.

Thomas Mann, by means of his detailed introduction, has given a central significance to this child songbird and to the power of music in general. All the other suggestions discussed by the brothers had been abandoned by them when they remembered the musical talents of the girl: "Take your zither and go on ahead of us, and sing loud and resoundingly that Joseph lives." Thus the language of music is shown to be more powerful and victorious than any other. Thomas Mann once wrote in his essay "Erziehung zur Sprache": "Der Ursprung des Wunsches, eine Sache siegreich auszudrücken, ist Liebe."[7] Her love for her grandfather as well as her love for her art and for the mission that has been so suddenly placed in her young hands gives Serach's song the power to prepare Jacob for a comprehension of the unbelievable news.

This "triumphant" function of music also explains the strange fact that, instead of using the one sentence of the song in the legend, Thomas Mann invented a long poem of many stanzas whose beginning bears a resemblance to the first lines of Psalm 96.

This very poetic and artistic song is the main digression from the old legend. To object to a twelve-year-old girl's producing such an artful song, especially in rhymed verses, which do not exist in biblical poetry, would be to take too realistic a viewpoint. The purpose of the song is to emphasize the symbolic character of the poetic message. The medieval legend mentions only in a cursory way that Serach "knew how to play on the harp." In Thomas Mann's novel, however, the whole lovely appearance of the girl is the embodiment of music.

Moving across the pastures toward the hills, Serach makes up the verses and the melody of her poetical message whose refrain runs: "Thy son's alive!" At first she produces only the two lines:

> Oh wondrous strange, for now the truth is plain
> That quite, quite otherwise it came to pass.

But soon she starts another version in irregular stanzas of varying lengths with alternating masculine and feminine rhymes.

The creation of the poem out of the rhythm of Serach's walking is also illustrated by the following episode: A shepherd who has been listening to Serach's song with astonishment approaches the girl and asks for information as to its meaning. Serach, however, turns away, for she does not wish the song growing in her to be interrupted. The shepherd then goes on with her and soon he and Serach are joined by a little troop of men, women, and children. "The children danced to the rhythm, the elders walked in the time of it; all their faces were turned to her, and she went on singing. . . ."

In this way Serach's musical creation finds an audience that is inspired by the rhythmical power of her verses. But whether Serach's talents are great enough to fulfill her mission is to be determined only at the end of her walk when she finally arrives in the presence of Jacob, her grandfather:

> For a word of beauteous rareness
> In my music interweaves,
> Matching all it hath of fairness,
> And it says: Thy darling lives!

However, Thomas Mann extends the rhythmical motif still further. The patriarch himself, moved by the sweet-sounding voice of his granddaughter, starts to clap his hands to the rhythm of the song until, comprehending its inherent meaning, he becomes bewildered and lets his hands fall.

From now on the character of Jacob regains the mythical stature it has in the first volume of Mann's series of novels. As Israel he bears the name of his people and represents its conscience. Therefore, he warns Serach to follow the commands of the Lord and not to be tempted by false pagan gods. "For God is a high and difficult task, but 'the Gods' are a pleasant sin." The girl, however, does not interrupt her singing. The end of her song coincides with the joyous cries of the gathering household, indicating the return of Jacob's sons, who shortly thereafter appear in front of their father.

III

This indeed is a presentation much richer in human and epic elements than the medieval legend. Mann's story achieves its greatest depth and dramatization when the tremendously excited old man addresses his sons: "I am tempted to welcome your coming solely because I count on you to protect me from this child and the lying tongue her music has, since I know you would not allow my gray hair to be mocked." But the answer is the shouting of the assembled crowd: "The truth!" After Benjamin, the youngest of the brothers, has recounted what had happened in Egypt, Jacob blesses his granddaughter, praying, as in the legend, that the girl "shall not taste death but go living into the kingdom of heaven."

This blessing, at this point of the plot, gives the story a religious climax. Later the dramatic tension is lightened by a humorous touch. Jacob wants to learn whether Joseph has not become too corpulent in Egypt, a question that his son Juda smilingly denies.

The end of the chapter is similar to its beginning. Serach, the little maid, is sitting once more alone in the meadow under the wide blue sky. Her mission has been fulfilled: "All was but a Godlike jest."

In spite of its individualistic character, this episode is closely connected with the whole many-sided narrative of Joseph and his brothers. In this work of Thomas Mann's, Jacob and Joseph embody two historical types: the ancestor represents the mythical-religious type of man; Joseph, however, is the first modern individualist. To be sure, he never forgets his origin, but he becomes worldly and somewhat estranged from his ancestral tradition. His father had always thought of Joseph as of a beautiful boy who had been the victim of wild beasts. Yet now he was said to be the ruler of Egypt! "If he had not lived he would not be living. Blessed be the name of the Lord!"

For Jacob, Joseph, the man of the future, remains the boy of the past. The end of the novel reunites father and son. Thus the timeless character of the story is reestablished. "The essence of life is presentness, and only in a mythical sense does its mystery appear in the time-forms of past and future."[8]

NOTES

1. *Dichtung und Wahrheit*, Bk. 4, pt. 1, Jubiläums-Ausgabe, 22:165.
2. The best known collection is the Hebrew *Sefer ha-Jachar* ("Book of Honest People"), an anonymous edition of biblical legends. A printed edition appeared in Venice in 1630.
3. Micha Josef bin Gorion, therefore, edited the Joseph stories under the title *Joseph und seine Brüder: Ein altjüdischer Roman*, Berlin, 1938. The latest English edition of Jewish legends appeared under the title *The Legends of Israel*. Translated from the Hebrew of I. B. Levner by Joel Snowman, vol. 1: *From the Creation to the Death of Joseph*, With foreword by Cecil Roth (London, 1946).
4. Hugo von Hofmannsthal once wrote about the creative significance of the biblical subjects: "Nach außen hin setzen sie die Phantasie der Welt unabhängig in Bewegung, so dieser vom ägyptischen Joseph, an welchem, nach so vielen Musikern, Malern und Dichtern, auch Goethe nicht unberührt vorübergegangen ist." *Josephslegende*, Handlung von Harry Graf Kessler und Hugo von Hofmannsthal, Musik von Richard Strauss (Berlin, 1914), p. 11.
5. Snowman gave to this legend the title "Everlasting Life" (pp. 105 ff. of his edition). In bin Gorion's edition it is the 39th chapter (pp. 75 ff.).
6. In the German edition "Verkündigung"—*Joseph der Ernährer* (Stockholm, 1943), pp. 504 ff.; American edition: *Joseph the Provider* (New York, 1944), pp. 323 ff.
7. *Rede und Antwort* (Berlin, 1922), p. 369.
8. *Joseph and His Brothers* (New York, 1945), 1:54.

The Nature and the Work of Martin Buber

(On the Occasion of His Eightieth Birthday, February 8, 1958)

> The true community is the Sinai of the future.
> —Martin Buber

I

Our memories, too, change.

In years past, when we thought back to the First World War, that time appeared to us as a sad, painful, bloody episode that we were able to overcome. Today we know that it was the beginning of the decline whose victims we became.

Martin Buber recognized earlier and more profoundly than others that the foundations of our European existence had become questionable and fragile. He saw the crises in society, in education, in religion, in philosophy, and in our existence as Jews. In a series of monographs entitled *Die Gesellschaft* [Society] he assembled sociologists and philosophers for a critical investigation of the foundations of the epoch. In 1916 he founded the periodical *Der*

Rudolf Kayser and Martin Buber, 1957

Jude [The Jew] as an independent organ that was to be devoted to all intellectual concerns of Jewry.

In an age that was still under the spell of positivism and the exact sciences, Buber the philosopher had the courage to be a metaphysician, perhaps the only genuine metaphysician in the German-speaking world. Books like *Daniel: Dialogues on Realization, I and Thou*, and the collection *Ekstatische Konfessionen* attempted to restore the eternal problems of existence beyond the empirical world to the center of philosophy, from which Kant had banished them.

In those days many people came to believe that Buber was a mystic. But a mystic is aloof from life and the world, while Buber always addresses himself to the here and now. He believes in the unity between the self and the world, of experience and reality. What we experience is not our I, but always a Thou. The forlornness and isolation of modern man, his lack of a Thou, are his greatest misfortune. The "primary words" of the language are *I, Thou*, and *It*. Without a feeling of community we can neither live nor fight. This feeling determines the direction of our existence as thinking persons.

The reality of the community is our old Jewish heritage, but the feeling for it had become weaker and weaker in recent generations. We had become old and frail. Reforms in the synagogue and the struggle of the factions brought no help, and Zionism appeared to be a political utopia. People did not want any ties; they did not wish to be limited by traditions and memories that blocked a wide view. Their sense of life and feeling of space and freedom resembled that of the German Romanticist Clemens Brentano:

> So weit als die Welt,
> So mächtig der Sinn,
> So viel Fremde er umfangen hält,
> So viel Heimat ist ihm Gewinn.*

And then came the terrible awakening.

---

*Our minds are as strong as the world is wide. To the extent that we embrace foreign lands will we gain a home.

Fioretti of St. Francis of Assisi, a work to which they are superior in seriousness and profundity. The style of these tales has the luminosity and colorfulness of chiaroscuro, and in its images and rhythms it displays the kind of poetic mastery that has become quite rare in our age.

Buber regards the Hasidim, an Eastern Jewish sect that came into being around the middle of the eighteenth century, as the only Jewish movement of the postbiblical period in which the elemental religious feeling of primitive times breaks through once more. Through anecdotes and legends, wise sayings, and invocations of God, Hasidism reached the people, forming communities and heightening the communal spirit. "A legend," says Buber, "is the myth of I and Thou, of the called and the caller, of the finite one who enters infinity and the infinite one who needs the finite." A scorned and buried religious world has been wrested from oblivion by Buber's free re-creation.

This is the rich, incomparable harvest of the octogenarian thinker. These are the gardens through which he leads us with kindly hands. Here I can only briefly indicate this multiplicity that the misfortune of our age has brought closer to many of us than in earlier years.

More than forty years ago Gustav Landauer wrote about Buber's work, which has since then greatly expanded and stood the test of time. Landauer's words have only now attained their full validity: "He issued no appeal, did not tell people to be ashamed, nor did he call for understanding, tolerance, or humanitarianism. He simply spoke to the Jews in public, and by giving them a comprehensive picture of the past, which he transfigured and almost fashioned into a myth, he told them from the depth of his own soul what it meant that they were Jews."

(translated by Harry Zohn)

In Memory of Franz Kafka
(1946)

> Dreams have arrived; they have come upstream and climb up the embankment wall on a ladder. People stop and converse with them; the dreams know many things, but not where they have come from.
>
> —Kafka

I

It has been more than twenty years since Franz Kafka died at the age of forty of consumption of the larynx.

He was a person of great shyness, timid toward life, lonely, a doubter, and very serious. From his youth on he had a constant companion: his death. For this death lasted many years; it moved toward him and away from him, taking him to hospitals and sanatoriums. Sometimes it seemed to leave him altogether, and then it returned with new threats, like a stormy evening after a Spring day. Shortly before it conquered him, death used a strange ruse to cheat its victim: the man of forty assumed the appearance of a twenty-year-old. He was now quite youthful and began to trust life. It was when he was publishing his collection of stories, *A Hunger Artist*, and eagerly studying Hebrew and the Talmud. But then his life quickly came to an end. "You can't stay here," said the world to Franz Kafka, using his words from his novel *The Castle*.

Perhaps it was this profound acquaintance with death that made Kafka a citizen of two worlds, the earthly and the unearthly. "A man cannot live without an enduring trust in something indestructible in himself, though he may all his life be unaware of that indestructible thing and his trust in it." In faith in a personal God he sees one of the ways in which this lack of awareness may express itself, but there are many of them. Dreams, too, the true origin of which no psychology can reveal, tell us about this indestructible, enduring thing in the great flux of events, and they reveal and conceal at the same time. "The German word *sein* signifies both things: to be, and to belong to Him," said Kafka. This is the deepest and simplest formula for the two worlds in which we live. Being captive in the everyday world produces fear for the world and for life. We must capture our freedom by expanding the spheres of our existence. There are so many steps between us and God. What matters is never the self but always the greater existence of which it is part. "In the struggle between you and the world, back the world." And if it is stronger than you, you must not attempt to cheat it out of its victory.

One is tempted to speak of a kind of psychological (*inner-worldly*, to use Max Weber's term) asceticism that is the basic feature of Kafka's thinking and writing. Precisely because he knows all about the problems of his self, because he closely observes himself in all his encounters with the world, and because the anxiety in him and around him must not overwhelm him, he yearns for objectivity and commitment. When he was working on his novel *Amerika*, he wrote in his diary: "How I hold on to my novel against all restlessness, much like a figure on a monument that looks into the distance while holding on to its pedestal." Do not give yourself up, even if redemption never comes—that is the maxim of Kafka's life. But in that profound paradox which governs existence always and everywhere, those who do not wish to give themselves up must transform themselves and integrate themselves in the communities of men, things, nature, and God. Only this transformation into objectivity keeps us alive as subjects.

In the diaries, notebooks, and letters of Franz Kafka, those prodigious sources for the revelation of his essential nature, he always speaks about this one great paradox. Whether we sit around a family table, whether we read, write, talk, listen, or pray (writing is a "form of prayer," too), we transform ourselves, stepping out of our selves and into other worlds. If we can no longer do this, our deepest essence is in danger. Instead of looking at the world through a window, we look into a mirror and thus at ourselves. But as we do so, we put a distance between the observing and the observed self. We divide and dismember ourselves between the conscious and the unconscious. We would like to see our seeing eye. Kafka says in such a case that he has become suspicious of himself and is scared. It happens only occasionally, but it disturbs him.

It is incomprehensible to him, though it is evidence of a blessed superabundance of strength, if someone in pain is able to objectivize that pain. Anyone who does this does not transform himself; he remains in his condition, can talk about it, can in his painful misfortune write to someone that he is unhappy, and can put many variations on this theme on paper; and yet his pain is genuine and great. Certainly it takes an abundance of strength, but who can manage to muster it?

At the bed of a child, sitting opposite the mother, we feel: "It no longer depends on you—unless you desire it." This was at all times Franz Kafka's sense of life. But if it does depend on me because I desire it and because cheerfulness and energy command it, then the decision must produce great results; then I shall come out of my self as victor, and the superabundance of my vitality objectivizes itself in the realms above and outside myself: objects, dreams, and faith. Only in this way can a person really write: with complete surrender of his body and his soul to the world and to mankind.

"Theoretically there is a perfect possibility for happiness: to believe in the indestructible element in oneself and not strive after it." Here we see a relationship between Franz Kafka and Heinrich von Kleist, for whom it is a prerequisite of grace that knowledge has, as it were, passed through infinity. But who among us knows the supreme happiness of the spirit's being able to hold free sway and no longer having to be the support of a frail self, so that, in Kleistian terms, a person has returned to a state of innocence? In this state we need not make ourselves small; we *are* small and belong to the universe. But if that is not the case, we must do it; it is a beginning, a deed.

II

Is this a philosophy?

It is the substance of Franz Kafka from which all his works come. They are parables of this substance. It would therefore be wrong to interpret them psychologically and trace them back to the writer's experiences. Goethe, too, liked to call himself "an old maker of parables," who translated his substance into the objective language of words and inventions. Much has been written about Kafka's reality symbolism, but what is actually symbolized has usually been overlooked. It is not individual, accidental phenomena, but existence itself. That is why Kafka seeks to make his self small, to make it disappear, to dissolve the destructible in the indestructible the way a powder is dissolved in a liquid. In one's work this is possible; in one's life it remains an unattainable ideal.

This is why Kafka is less concerned with the figures in his stories than with their lives in general. Each individual life symbolizes the totality of existence. This is a point of contact between Kafka, Goethe, and Kierkegaard. (Kafka said about Kierkegaard that his case was similar to his own: "At least he is on the same side of the world.") This symbolism is more than a mere literary form; it is a way of looking at life. Nevertheless, Kafka is a precise realist who knows how to describe all the details of life—offices, attics, schoolrooms, inns, and their everyday inhabitants, all the little destructible things of the here and now. But what is revealed through them is the indestructible, the incomprehensible: God.

In the novels *The Castle* and *The Trial*, the main figure is named simply K. This figure is devoid of individuality, an anonymous bearer of qualities. But K. also has occupations; in one case he is a bank clerk, in the other a land surveyor, and in both occupations he struggles against imaginary authorities and fights for things that effectively constitute the substance of his life: an unknown guilt that he once incurred. In these uncanny contests with invisible adversaries there is symbolized the duality of existence, the tension between the destructible and the indestructible, which is as mysterious for us as the castle is for the village and the court for the accused man.

This dualism of existence is given expression at every opportunity. Everything we do has these two sides, usefulness and uselessness, and it is event and expression at once. The little mysteries of everyday life constitute the real contents of Kafka's legends and are the revelations of the indestructible, which we see constantly and everywhere—provided we are willing to see them. Like the emperor of China, the indestructible is great "through all levels of the world."

In *The Trial* a girl observes a man "raising his hands toward her and rubbing them together in supplication." Such an expressive movement, so touching in its simple vividness, must not be interpreted psychologically or traced back to an experience that logically and temporally preceded it. The movement is simply there as a very natural process the only decisive thing about which is that someone raises his hands toward another person in supplication. A feeling comes out of the self, transcends its limits, and tries to impart itself to another human being. It is the same longing for community that prevails in the fragment *The Great Wall of China:* "Unity! Unity! Shoulder to shoulder, a ring of people, blood no longer confined within the narrow circulation of the body but sweetly rolling and yet returning through endless China."

From without and from within, the indestructible bursts in upon the self, just as St. Augustine taught the unity of *Deus exterior et interior*. In the novel *The Castle* K. reflects on the landlady: "A born intriguer who seems to work senselessly, like the wind, on distant, strange orders one never gets to see." Thus the destructible is always determined by the indestructible, which we never get to see, and that is why the stories about it are legends—parables in the real world about the power of the unreal. In his Angel Sermon of 1831, Cardinal Newman said this about the angels: "Every breath of air and ray of light and heat, every beautiful prospect is, as it were, the skirts of their garments, the waving of the robes of those whose faces see God in heaven."

Thus all phenomena of life come from the indestructible. This constitutes their value as symbols. What matters is only from what side one looks at them. Even Satan was a fallen angel, and evil is part of God's plan for the world. K., too, has incurred some guilt, and that is why he is subject to the mysterious court against which he cannot prevail. Christianity's redemption in the hereafter does not beckon to him; rather, he has to shoulder the sorrow of his guilt as well as the sufferings of the world, which it is futile to flee. "You can keep away from the sorrows of the world; you are free to do so and it is in keeping with your nature, but perhaps this very keeping away is the only sorrow you could avoid."

This is the baroque world of Franz Kafka.

(translated by Harry Zohn)

Jakob Wassermann

> The longing for the creative is lodged deeper in the soul of the Jew than in any other race; the longing for the creator—it finds its explanation in the intimate religious feeling of the Jew.
> —Jakob Wassermann

I

Parting from a friend—that parting which leaves no hope—arouses in us an emotion too deep to permit of an evaluation of only his literary work. Wassermann's works to me are pictures of his human soul. When taking leave of his friend Hugo von Hofmannsthal, he said, "It must frighten us to grow older; one after another they pass away; if you look back, you see a cemetery, and the tombstones of those who have left first are already weatherbeaten." He also is now at rest who restlessly loved life, absorbed the present and transformed the past into living experience. His art renders all the conflicts, motives, adventures, and all the hazards in his soul. In all its abundance and manifoldness this art is his world. In this world his experiences are converted into new realities, which no longer betray the secluded inquietude out of which they grew. In this world there prevail the storms, fears, and good fortunes of a spiritual life, which began at an early age and also ended soon; Jakob Wassermann did not grow old.

This world, conceived by the conflict with the ego, reacted upon the author in such a way as to dominate him. This domination "could be overcome only by opposing to it a personality which could always resist the lure of the new creation."

Thus, every new work gave him opportunity to test his conscience and to improve himself. He never severed the spirit from poetical life but permitted his life to be borne by it. It was his transcendence. The spirit and the life are always related to each other, just as are art and nature. In this sense art is a simile for life and the spirit. Wassermann said: "And if I do not realize the similitude, I am but a poor fool who wishes to sell the people stones for bread." But it was bread he gave, both in his art and in his friendship.

He lived for both, for his work and his friends belonged to him just as he belonged to them. In both he unfolded the world of his emotions, of his thoughts and his visions. How else could a man feel who saw all creative reality in man, in the indelible impression of acquaintances, which dominate all existence? We—and he, too—hoped that the fertility of such encounters might last much longer. Then the world in which he enjoyed life and fame changed; he arrived at his last encounter, the encounter with death.

The consideration of a man who has parted from us is always associated with the events and experiences that united him with us. I met Jakob Wassermann every year and even toward the end—a few weeks before his death. Our last conversation concerned his health. "I have just come from the hospital—gall colic and arthritis. We shall meet again." These words frightened me but I did not surmise that I now heard this veiled, soft, slightly South-German voice for the last time.

As I delve into the folds of my memory, I recall accidental conversations and encounters which, to be sure, always revealed the innermost aspects of his human soul. It is more than a decade ago that we met in Munich and spent some unforgettable winter days together. Wassermann proved his friendship to me in many ways; he told me about his youth, which he had spent in this city. He spoke of his hard struggle for existence and his painful ascent. I also recall our discussion of his plan of a revision of his novel *Christian*

Wahnschaffe [*The World's Illusion*]. He had taken this work up again and felt dissatisfied; it seemed to him overburdened with minor details, exaggerations, and irrelevancies. He used a drastic comparison: "This novel is like a goose with too much fat. One must cut away the fat to make the meat palatable." With this in mind he undertook the revision.

Wassermann was always completely absorbed in his work. A friend said of him: "He must sit at his desk—that is where he lives." His work was the mirror in which he sought himself and out of which the faces of his characters peered at him. They were the faces of his dreams, the metamorphoses of his experiences, the world of his characters, the world of his finder's luck. This finder's luck particularly distinguished him. Epic fantasy, to be sure, is different from simple imagery, from the invention of actions and people, from adventuring among arbitrary occurrences. The poet transforms the real world into the fantastic and dispels charms to reveal the human.

He saw in life a fantastic abundance spread out before him as in a beautiful garden. He distributed it again in his novels. To this end he needed experiences, but they had to be transformed into the other reality, that of poetry. He himself related how his material developed into poetic works. One must not compare the power of destiny in his characters and ideas with the facts of reality. This power becomes overawing only when through it the fate-element in the narrative is fulfilled. The real facts were for him only a structure, the theme was only the base for the transformed life that is depicted in the novel. How narrow-minded, how utterly wrong is it, therefore, to insist on a research for the material inspiration. "For, there was an infinite number of metamorphoses which the original picture had to undergo, so that the final picture had only that in common with the first one which the block of ore has in common with the statue." In this sense the poet does not invent; he finds meaning and form. He must have the experience of reality, but this reality is composed of the observations of our senses and the ties and secrets of our soul. The facts are at the beginning; the end gives us his world of poetry and its characters.

II

In his conversations and essays, the character was Wassermann's favorite theme. In it he saw the individually limited figure and the metamorphosis of man through fantasy. The mass can never be personified. The social fate can never manifest itself in the novel in any other way than through the fate of the individual, regardless of the ties that exist between it and the mass. Through complicated spiritual or social relations, each individual is tied to all the others. "Besides those things which it reveals to us, the individual always hints at some secrets concerning itself. The more secrets relating to certain ties or seemingly conflicting qualities it suggests, the more (through stimulation of the imagination) does it take on corporeality in the mind of the observer or reader." The poet looms as the last secret behind the secret of his characters. They are never identical, but they always meet again in spite of the differences between them. It is this difference that presupposes the individual limitation and the strangeness of the individual as it is perceived by the mass. "Some see blue, others see black, the majority sees stupid," says Flaubert.

Wassermann had full command of the technique of novel-writing. There is high tension, crime, and adventure; there is history, landscape, and the family. We find virtue, grandeur and sin, passion, power and sickness, state and society. Life rules in its greatness and in its insignificance. These novels do not depict that superficial naturalism of observation and experimentation. They do not give an analysis of given conditions. They are full of world-experience and of life-experience. That Wassermann was most prolific in the field of the novel is not only the result of his predilection for this kind of literature or of his great narrative ability;

it is rather his world-experience and his understanding of the human soul, which lead him to that form of writing in which the most subtle and analytic thoughts can be best expressed.

His fantasy was as blessed as that of the oriental teller of fairy tales, and men and women of all callings and people of every generation listened to him. Each one finds a gate to Wassermann's world and, among the hundreds of characters that live in his novels and tales, each one of his readers finds one that is closely related to his own experiences and fate.

Is this close relationship dependent upon the epoch? "That I live in my time is my fate" says the "man of forty years." Surely there exist internal and external circumstances that are different today from what they were yesterday. But in human life there exists a kind of happiness and disappointment, of longing and of satisfaction that is not peculiar to a certain period but rather to a particular kind of people. Goethe once said, "It would be sad, indeed, if each one of us, at one time or another in his life, would not have passed through an epoch in which it seemed to him that *Werther* was written especially for him." Wassermann emphasized that the creative ability of a man depended on how much of his youth was still in him. "Everything young and everything old" he says in the preface to *Caspar Hauser*. It is impossible to speak of a clear and homogeneous development in Wassermann. His faith in art, however, his mental unrest, and his acute realization of what is right and humane are homogeneous. Out of this faith evolves his great enemy—inertia of the heart. With it is concerned not only his novel *Caspar Hauser* but also his entire work. He poses the human heart against the whole world, and Caspar's purity, as heaven against the sinister earth. If one assumes that positive and loving attitude toward life, one must perceive that life buds even out of sin. "Innocent, my dear, is God alone." These are the final words of *Caspar Hauser*.

Becoming accustomed to the insufficient, to the puny selfishness of weak minds; to be satisfied with one's little private troubles and to renounce the suffering of the world—all this is inertia of the heart. To fall prey to it is the saddest and most general fate. Who has the courage to become an adventurer out of his sense of responsibility? In *Das Gaensemaennchen* we read: "Don't you believe that you carried the sorrow of the world; your own you have carried, lovingly-loveless, unselfishly-selfish, monster that you were, a social creature!" The inertia of the heart leads away from fate, its odor, its momentum, its intensity. "It grows or withers like the plant; it attracts or repulses other fates, as it sees fit; it is above man, for a while or for a thousand years, as it sees fit, then it is in man." This realist Wassermann is also a poet of faith. Humaneness, for him, is not social happiness but redemption from the ego. That man steps out of his glass-bell and no longer perceives the image of others refracted and dulled—that is real humaneness. Redemption is liberation from the prison of the ego. This faith determines also Wassermann's views concerning the great questions of the epoch. He does not try to evade them. He hates the formless "anarchists of mind." He also conceives of form as a moral principle. "One must conceive of form as an expression of the divinity, as a symbol of the complete circle, perfect in itself. It provides the only protection against the horror of eternity and the darkness of death, which stare at us from every direction. To live differently is impossible." Wassermann often presents his moral convictions in an oversimplified dialectic method through characters that represent faith and faithlessness, construction and destruction, nature and reason. He himself points to these pairs of contrasts in his novels: Agathon and Gudstikker, Alexander and Arrhidaeos, Caspar Hauser and Quandt, Nothafft and Philippine, Christian and Niels Engelschall, Etzel and Waremme. In the acuteness of their enmity, in the battle of self-sustenance, in deceptions and truths, they attempt to break through the glass-wall of their ego. Such stresses dominate the internal forces of reality and create the tragedies and forebodings. But activity will out. It penetrates everyday life and nature. "All action, good and evil, flows through all nature," we read in *Christian Wahnschaffe*.

III

The abundance of Wassermann's characters is immeasurable. They are derived from all social strata and provinces of the soul.

Thus these novels, taken as a whole, render a "Comédie humaine" in the sense of Balzac. They call Wassermann a realist and a psychologist. Can a novelist be anything but that? There was a time when people thought they had to combat the psychological novel and overlooked that human passion, urges, and thoughts could not be rendered any other way than psychologically. Psychology does not imply a specific method, but rather a standard by which the most diverse experiences are measured. All of Wassermann's characters agree with Agathon: "To be gracious means everything." They follow truth, and truth is a moral ideal. Fantasy does not oppose it, but on the contrary, elevates truth. "The world of the poet is a world of examples. It has only one practical application; namely, transmutation." Thus fantasy goes hand in hand with moral faith, with the faith in humanity and justice.

One is tempted to organize this epic world by dividing it into groups. Yet every work stands isolated as an island, and yet it is always a development, proceeding from the course determined by the previous works. And yet they form a complete whole, for they are replenished by the same currents of thought. We have the group of fantastic and adventure novels, which are oriental in their visionary power and happy colorfulness. Most typical of this group, in my opinion, are the prelude to *Die Juden von Zirndorf, Der goldene Spiegel, Der Aufruhr um den Junker Ernst*—this most beautiful fruit of his maturity. We have the novels and biographies dealing with historical events in which the process of transition extends over centuries: *Alexander in Babylon, Die Schwestern, Caspar Hauser, Bula Matary, Christoph Columbus*. We have time-novels in which, however, time is something else than the external theme, but rather a definite spiritual situation or intellectual problem-situation: *Die Geschichte der jungen Renate Fuchs, Der Mann von vierzig Jahren, Das Gaensemaennchen, Christian Wahnschaffe, Der Wendekreis, Laudin und die Seinen*, and *Joseph Kerkhovens dritte Existenz*. And here we have the works of his moral mission, of his sense of justice and ethical rigor: *Der Moloch, Der Fall Mauritius, Etzel Andergast*. As in Heinrich von Kleist's Michael Kohlhaas, there flows out of the characters of these novels a burning sense of justice through one's heart. Justice—that is the great and most comprehensive postulate of religious mankind. The Jew Elassar pronounces it: "The law is here; the judges are also here, and also the books in which everything is written down. But justice? That is not here." To make justice victorious, even in one case only, which then would be an example for all the others, is a task that the boy Etzel Andergast sets for himself. He knows that this victory would serve to uphold not only an idea but also his own existence. "What does it import to know myself; what is justice if I cannot enforce it, I, myself, Etzel Andergast?" Here we are in the center of the moral faith of Jakob Wassermann. He had a very imaginative eye but even greater and more creative was his imagery of words. He considered the word "the most treacherous and most tempting element" we know. It determines the rhythm of the innermost being. It is the material from which the world of the mind and of the dreams is built up and it has been well known to the poet from eternity. Of language, Wassermann said: "It has formed my features, lit up my eyes, led my hand, directed my foot, made my nerves vibrate, my heart feel, and taught my brain to think."

He considers the German language the most precious spiritual heritage, the administration of which is a responsible undertaking and affords the greatest creative happiness. It gives balance to the imaginings of the mind, for it gives shape and form, meaning, and perception. It embodies all that is heard and seen, all dreams and their fulfillments, all the verve and experience of his life. If in his work he was led not only by his genius but also by his professional passion, it was because of his deep spiritual intimacy with the language, the German language, which he considered his holy heritage.

From this sense of responsibility Wassermann derived his untiring diligence. Johann Sebastian Bach used to say: "I had to be industrious. Whoever is just as industrious will be just as successful." The diligence of an artist is by no means the secret of his creativeness but it is a symbol of his sense of responsibility. Wassermann was the strictest judge of himself, and the printed books are sometimes the tenth or twentieth revisions of his original manuscripts. He looked back at the genesis of his works as one looks at an interesting biological process.

IV

Wassermann's creative work revolves about two foci, Germanism and Judaism. It is for this reason that he entitles his autobiography *My Road as a German and as a Jew*. His Judaism he conceived of as being an irksome problem as well as a faith, a fervor and a vision of a historical fate of world importance. When at the age of twenty-three he wrote *Die Juden von Zirndorf*, he reached "back to fundamental facts, to ancestry, to the myths and legends of a people, the descendant of which I had to consider myself, and on the other hand I wished to shape the growing life of this people in a mythical, very much simplified, very comprehensive sense." Judaism for him has the twofold meaning: past and present, fulfillment and the problematic.

He saw the undefined, unhappy situation of the Jews in the German sphere of life, to which, however, he clung with all his feeling and with his poet's fantasy. Thus he experienced in himself the discord and the uncertainty in the soul of the Jew of our time.

A solution of the Jewish problem he could not see, for it was not his intention to change a situation in which his own existence and his spiritual fate were rooted. Thus his Jewish descent was to him at the same time his pride and his humiliation, a mark of distinction and a stigma. "Exposed to these ceaseless impacts, forced to live in the sphere of friction between these two sensations, he must find his place. Thus it was with almost all Jews whom I have met and it is the deepest, most difficult, and most important part of the Jewish problem."

One may consider this medial position as obscured and unsatisfactory, as the product of an unsettled time, which today has vanished. Of more importance than the solution of such a problem, however, from the standpoint of one of the parties concerned, is the experiencing of this problem. Wassermann experienced it deeply from his earliest youth and this experience acted on him up to his last work. Because he cannot find a solution, he puts in its place hope and the old messianic faith: "Perhaps, however, there is still a future. Perhaps there is a possibility of hope. Perhaps there is a saviour, human or spiritual, here or over there, or on a bridge between the two places. Perhaps he has already sent out his forerunner."

The last secret of the Jewish fate remains inexplicable. It belongs to the elements of our existence—and the elementary remains forever inexplicable.

Moritz Heimann, 1868-1925

Even great men were to me not drinks but goblets.
—Moritz Heimann

There is no better word to characterize Moritz Heimann's essential nature than wisdom. To Plato wisdom was a virtue, thus not erudition but insight of the heart, *sapientia*. This virtue was expressed in Heimann's conversations even more than in his works; in fact, one is tempted to characterize his writings as conversations with invisible readers. In a soft voice and with manly kindness he led them through the labyrinth of life, which for him had two foci: his Germanness and his Jewishness.

"There is nothing unnatural about traveling one's orbit with two foci; a few comets do, and all the planets." To fathom this duality completely, one must have visited him in his Brandenburg village during his last years. In Kagel, an inaccessible village far removed from all highways, he lived among farmers in the house of his ancestors. Smilingly he explained: "This is where I studied Hebrew, this is where I learned to pray." And his return to this world of his fathers gave the ailing man peace and relief. Once he said something about Martin Buber that also applies to him: "He is a descendant of Jewish scholars with the pride of a grandson, and yet excited by the conscience of the future."

As a grandson of German Jewry Heimann did not live to see its downfall, nor did he comprehend the incipient changes in Europe and the world. "To base a nation on industry," he once said, "means to base it on something provisional." But industrialization is the common denominator of all the breaks and breakdowns that we are experiencing in our time. At bottom Heimann believed in what existed, in the continuation of yesterday. Thus he saw in Zionism only a utopia and regarded the idea that European Jews would ever give up their fatherlands as senseless. In later years he believed in a Jewish renewal through youth. He called the *halutzim*, young people who were seeking new shores, a source of pride and comfort: "Would anyone with a heart not feel it? And even if they are not pioneers of some daemon of an idea, they are pioneers of their own lives—admirable and enviable."

Heimann's style of thinking, speaking, and writing was of a simple clarity and humble selflessness. In this he appeared very North German and was akin to Kleist, Hebbel, and Fontane. His attitude toward nature was similar and in keeping with the harsh, somber quality of the North German plain. Hebbel once wrote in his diaries: "In nature everything is always together. In an organism nothing is added, nothing drops off, everything only develops." Heimann, too, was imbued with such a feeling for organic nature, and probably the strongest expression of this may be found in his novella *Wintergespinst* [Winter Yarn] in a description of a village street: "The paths sprout to all places, authentic, in accordance with theoretical principles, and irregular like branches of a tree. And everywhere there are villages, and houses line all the streets."

Southern gaiety and ironic playfulness were alien to his serious nature. Once this gave rise to a misunderstanding between us. It was in the years when every writer was trumpeting forth his convictions and elevating words to world-redeeming deeds. I smilingly remarked that his writings contained no "convictions." But because he did not notice my smile, he misunderstood my words as criticism and took some time to calm down again.

In everything he did Heimann was a seeker—a seeker after truth and after God. He saw the enigmas of existence, but he did not have the presumption to want to solve them; instead, he experienced them in pious humility. For him the most exalted knowledge was not to know what we are. "To sojourn under the sun and in his own spirit at the same time, and to recognize both over and over again as the same holy light"—this is how Oskar Loerke described Moritz Heimann's essential nature.

Many of his works concern themselves with Jews and Judaism. He was shaken by the ancient, wild restlessness of the Jewish people that has given rise to so many historical figures, legends, and bits of wisdom. In his drama *Das Weib des Akiba* the dying Akiba looks back on his life and his struggle: "Years, long years, a long dream, a long wakefulness! You will not reject my heart, O Lord, because it did not forget its wildness." Such a wild heart bears misfortune more easily than people who are content with good fortune. "For there is," Heimann writes in *Wintergespinst,* "a general sense of misfortune that makes us feel good, as though fate had no power over us now." One may regard such words as an avowal of Jewishness.

The imagery of Heimann's language dominates all of his writings. Heimann never uses philosophical terminology to formulate his thoughts, and in this he resembles Pascal and other moralists. In all creations he hears the message, which is the only thing that matters.

Heimann believes that one should not avoid the entanglements of life but should seek them out. This attitude often makes his writings difficult to read, though his language is always clear and very vivid. In moments of painful pensiveness it often takes on a lyrical quality and lets emotion take control of the intellect. Perhaps Heimann never wrote more visionary and yet thoughtful sentences than the ones with which the protagonist of his drama *Armand Carrel* beholds his doom from the window of his apartment and of his life: "A river by night to which no one gives a thought—coming from somewhere, gurgling around its little islands, flowing unseen and plaintively past its mountains; occasionally a boat travels on it with a light—and incessantly, never assuaged, it pushes and foams on its way. . . ."

This drama, whose material derives from the political history of France in the age of Louis-Philippe, is the most powerful of

Heimann's plays, and it has also been very effective on the stage. I remember its premiere at the Berlin State Theater in 1920 and the small gathering of close friends afterwards. Like a prophecy these words came from the stage into our present: "We will collect everything and confuse everything and derive profit even from the death of God." Heimann wrote his political play very differently from the pathos-filled tendentious writings of those years. In a duel between two Paris journalists it symbolizes the conflict between business policies and an idealistic mentality, between pure faith and capitalistic profit. This drama is political in that highest sense which for Heimann politics possesses: "to navigate between journalism and chiliasm in a prudent voyage." Carrel ventures such a voyage, which is bound to lead him to his death: "One must prepare for a longer period of time than a human being's life span."

Heimann's prose writings have been published in five volumes. They are the heritage, nearly forgotten today, of a generation that still found it possible to be optimistic and earnest at the same time. After his death appeared a collection entitled *Die Spindel*; the plays were issued separately. In all his works there is that clear, rhythmic, graphic language that ranges from the street corner to heaven. Heimann was fond of definitive, often surprising formulations. For example, he calls Tolstoy "this mountain range of a man," and in an essay about Taoism he confesses: "It is very hard for a less godly mouth to utter the truth of a godly one, no matter how lively a sense of this truth it may have."

This humble sense of life is oriented more toward the East than toward the West. Nature, too, is included in the intellectual realm, since it is the most powerful life-creating force. A farmer knows that the laws of living are not made by human beings but by the divine course of the seasons. Every individual represents all of nature; every tree is already a forest. This attitude also explains Heimann's warning not to overestimate the works of our intellect, because very few of these come up to what is really essential. One of his aphorisms reads: "We should not make more of any idea than it makes of us." He knew that, intellectually speaking, even a small number of houses, the sea, the sand, and the sky cannot be coped with in centuries. Like Adalbert Stifter he experienced the greatness of the small and the smallest things and loved them.

Heimann was the first literary adviser of the S. Fischer publishing house. When his illness forced him to slow down, he returned to his Brandenburg solitude, and Oskar Loerke took over his post. Heimann gave this publishing firm its original complexion, and he brought Gerhart Hauptmann (his brother-in-law), Hermann Stehr, Emil Strauss, Hermann Hesse, and many other authors into the fold. As a twenty-year-old in search of advice I was permitted to call on Heimann at his office, but I had no idea then that this house would become my home for many years.

In the hour of farewell all of us who had known, admired, and loved him stood mournfully at his feet, "which knew all the blessings and all the hardness of human paths, and close to his head which was a pure shelter for the image of this world, just as the world offered his head and his heart a beloved, infinite shelter" (Oskar Loerke at the funeral in the cemetery of the Jewish Community in Berlin-Weissensee).

(translated by Harry Zohn)

In Memoriam Albert Einstein

> When a person passes away, he takes a secret with him: how he in particular managed to live in a spiritual sense.
> —Hugo von Hofmannsthal

I

We call our departed the transfigured. Just as their rigidified features become clear and pure, freed from sorrows and joys, our memories of them become clear and pure as well. We see them as transfigured forms.

And yet there is one question that remains forever unanswered: the question as to that uncanny, mysterious force that gave form and meaning to a life that has been concluded, that made the departed person different from all others and surrounded him or her with a solitude that remained impenetrable even to those who thought they understood the person best. Our language can never describe a human being exactly, and it is impossible ever to coin a formula for him or her that possesses permanent validity. No one can say why a life took precisely the direction it did and why it was made happy or unhappy by these very experiences.

Only great and truly creative achievements are capable of illuminating the mystery of a human being to some extent. In such

Rudolf Kayser and Albert Einstein in the late thirties

achievements the same inner forces are at work as in life itself. And no matter how objective these achievements may be, even though they may have an independent life of their own or obey the strict laws of a science, enough personal elements remain to render the profoundest essence of the person's creativity and genius perceptible.

It is in this sense that Kant speaks of genius as "the peculiar spirit which a person is imbued with at birth, the protecting and guiding spirit that inspired those original ideas."

This protecting and guiding inspiration is the real genius of Albert Einstein, the substance of his life. He often concerned himself with the problem of the nature and the motivation of scientific research. In a speech made on the occasion of Max Planck's sixtieth birthday he said: "Man tries to make for himself in the fashion that suits him best a simplified and intelligible picture of the world; he then tries to some extent to substitute this cosmos of his for the world of experience, and thus to overcome it. This is what painters, poets, speculative philosophers, and natural scientists do, each in his own fashion. Each makes this cosmos and its construction the pivot of his emotional life, in order to find in this way the peace and security which he cannot find in the narrow whirlpool of personal experience."

II

Only seldom has this proximity of science and art, reason and emotion, self-control and firmness been experienced by anyone as strongly as it was experienced by Einstein. The experience of law and form as the forces capable of overcoming the cruel haphazardness of the daily hustle and bustle aroused an almost religious humility in him. Thus the music of Johann Sebastian Bach, the great master of form, was artistic perfection for him, while he had no taste for psychological analysis and naturalistic description of everyday life. The ideal he set up for the scientist was similar to the one he posed for the artist: "The supreme task of the physicist is to arrive at those universal elementary laws from which the cosmos can be built up by pure deduction."

The cosmos . . . The transformation of restless earthly reality into pure, eternal ideality; the "preestablished harmony" of Leibniz and the intellectual monism of Spinoza; lawfulness as the highest triumph over the presumptuousness of anarchic chance and arbitrariness—all that is Einstein's protecting and guiding spirit, the source of his scientific achievement and of his humanity. What has been called his aloofness from his times and his unworldliness has its true foundation and justification in this belief in the superpersonal power of a lawfully ordered world. Even our own selves are insignificant and unimportant in the face of that higher universality which can also be called God.

In an address to the students of the University of California, Einstein said: "If someone talks about scientific matters, the little word 'I' should not loom large in his exposition. But if he speaks about objectives and aspirations in science, he should be permitted to deal with himself. For there is no aspiration and no desire which a person experiences as directly as he does his own. In my own case, my aspirations were directed primarily at logical uniformity in physics."

This striving for universal uniformity, which is also the basis of monotheism, produced both Einstein's theory of relativity and his ethical-humanitarian *Weltanschauung*. The uniformity of the universe, deduced in strict mathematical formality, constitutes not only a clear model of nature that brings order into the colorful and contradictory empirical world but also the overcoming of the ego and the cares of everyday life.

III

Such an attitude may be called religious, for the essence of religion is not belief in a personal God but devotion to a higher totality on which we feel dependent—in the universe, within ourselves, in human society, and in the world of values.

This is why Einstein avowed: "My religiosity consists in a humble admiration of the infinitely superior spirit which reveals itself in the few aspects of reality that we are able to recognize with our feeble, infirm reason. Morality is a most important thing—but for us, not for God."

The visions of the world that physics had put forward over the years had not been able to develop an integral theoretical uniformity of the universe. Kant doubted if our reason would ever be capable of finding out "whether in the innermost part of nature that is unknown to us there is a connection between the physico-mechanical and the utilitarian relationships among objects in accordance with a certain principle."

The venture of such a unifying view of nature in the area of physics began with the special theory of relativity, proceeded to the general theory of relativity, and thence to a general field theory. In aesthetics, too, unity in variety is a foremost precept. In conversation Einstein was fond of using the word *"schön"* [beautiful] to designate a satisfactory solution of a problem.

IV

The first and perhaps the greatest difficulty that had to be overcome in this unification of nature was the problem of motion. Newton's absolutistic view had been contested over and over again, from Leibniz to Mach. Einstein found the Copernican solution by combining in his theory of motion space and time into a continuum and creating a still higher unity by combining this four-dimensional space-time continuum with gravitation. Space and time, mass and energy, inertia and gravitation, magnetism and electricity: all these elementary concepts that it had taken centuries to develop were now given a new and simplified meaning as links in a chain and building blocks of a comprehensive theory of the universe. Now the architect of this great and wide edifice confessed that he derived the strength for this from a certain faith: "What underlies all these endeavors is faith that the structure of what exists displays perfect harmony.

Today we have less reason than ever to let ourselves be diverted from this wonderful faith."

This wonderful faith remained with Einstein in his daily life as well. It gave him the strength to endure hostility, fame, disappointment, admiration, and hate. It also shaped his conviction that moral laws are valid in the social and political life of men.

Thus Einstein made himself a humble, personally unassuming servant of a higher harmony. He became a fighter whenever he saw the highest privilege demanded by such a faith violated: freedom of thought and of moral action.

Anyone who was privileged to share his life for decades experienced the blessing of an exemplary creative genius and a pious servant of the works of the spirit.

(translated by Harry Zohn)

PART III
Religion and Philosophy

Thoughts on Religion

We never finish with the ultimate problems. They always return transformed, and we can but respond with the same inadequate answers. The more distant from the practical needs of the moment the ultimate questions seem to be, the more eternal in nature they are, the more impossible is the attempt to arrive at a "definitive" solution. Nevertheless, the spiritual cares caused us by the ultimate questions are conditioned by the situation in which we experience them. The situation determines our choice of the answers from which we must choose and the form in which we give these answers.

I

Our age has brought about a radical transformation of all the conventional orders of human life. A tremendous process of transformation is threatening the social, political, and spiritual values to which we have attached our existence. The nihilistic catastrophe poses this question: Are there still other orders and values to which we can attach our lives so that they do not become prey to anarchy and futility? The decline of the traditions of human history focuses attention anew on a basically different world, which lies beyond human reality. The disappointment about its transitory character awakens a longing for ties that are independent of all the adventures of time. Only such a tie to timeless forces can free us from a destructive and unfruitful dependence upon a declining age.

However, this longing to conquer time through eternity, crisis through enduring laws, and evaluations through immutable values is of a religious nature. Indeed, the personal experience of the smallness, the inadequacy, and the inconstancy of human creations is the true essence of all religiosity. In religion man no longer feels himself to be the center, but placed between infinity and nothingness. Or in Pascal's words: "Car enfin qu'est-ce que l'homme dans la nature? Un néant à l'égard de l'infini, un tout à l'égard du néant, un milieu entre rien et tout."*

Religiosity has always been the experience that the eternal, infinite reality of existence is greater and mightier than the small reality of space and time in which we happen to live. Such a fundamental experience is the basis of all religious doctrines and systems. It is the source; the doctrine is merely the vessel from which we drink. Religiosity is the creative process in man from which religion arises as a creation. Religion is the basic decision to believe in a higher world than the human one and to lead and shape our lives in accordance with this belief. Religiosity always points toward the same direction beyond the so-called reality of man and increasingly tries to free him from this reality. It is a purely psychic fact, while the religious creations that it produces are dependent on the cultural and social situations in which they arose and which modified them. In other words: religiosity is a certain quest that has been an essential part of human nature in all ages and peoples. For this reason it is timeless. Religions, however, have their history, like all creations that originated in certain historical moments.

Religious man, who experiences the inadequacy of human orders and suffers because of it, always establishes bonds with higher orders by searching, questioning, and willing. The different religions have prepared different goals and answers, but these all lie more or less beyond the physical world and therefore remain unfathomable and mysterious in their ultimate ideas. For that

---

*"For, after all, what is man in nature? Nothing in regard to the infinite, everything in regard to nothingness; a middle between nothing and everything."

reason, the strength of the bond with the religious world lies not in the objects but in our subjective belief, which overcomes the smaller reality in order to gain the greater one.

Every religion wants to convey a total cosmic system and therefore seeks to embrace and regulate all experiences. But philosophy, science, and art also pursue the same goal and describe the total reality in which we live in their special languages. All of them, however, relate to man and can explain or shape the world only insofar as it can be experienced by us. Thus conceptions of the universe come into existence which, even if they strive for maximum objectivity, always apply to the human subject that created them. The world view of philosophy is always the conception of the philosopher; the way the natural sciences view the world is always bound to specific methods that were invented and developed by men. In other words, these conceptions of the universe have not only been created by man's reasoning or graphic imagination but are also to be comprehended only by men and are valid only for them. To a person who cannot think philosophically, philosophy cannot convey a conception of the universe. And in the same way, the scientific and artistic views of the universe remain mute and empty if they are not taken up by people who are scientifically educated or artistically gifted. Thus, in all comprehensive views of the world, man himself is the true prerequisite.

The cosmic system of religion, however, recognizes no such prerequisite. It aspires beyond human reality, not in order to enlarge it or to make conquests for the human spirit, but quite the contrary: in the comprehensive religious conception of the world, the reality in which we live is but a modest part of a greater entity. Since this entity exceeds our imagination, it cannot be perceptible to man. We can only surmise, love, and venerate the religious world order, but we cannot understand and explain it, just as a small joint can never survey the entire body to which it belongs.

In contrast to all those conceptions of the universe which are determined by human character, the religious conception demands from the outset that man renounce the idea of explaining and controlling the totality of existence through his qualities and abilities. Thus, the first fact in all religions is the acknowledgment that there are higher and mightier worlds than the limited one of man. Even though we may be creators in our human reality, in the higher world we are only creatures. From the psychological viewpoint, too, religious behavior is basically different from any other. Here we are not active, but we readily accept dependence on destiny. We do not strive for dominance, are not guided by our will to power, but we want to serve and be humble. We are conscious of the fact that the small partial reality in which we live and that we are able to recognize is dependent on an unknown, higher will that controls the greater reality of all existence.

Because the religious view of the world is completely different from all conceptions that are conditioned by the qualities that man himself possesses, that is, reason or imagination, it cannot be given expression. Religious experience cannot be expressed in the language of human reason nor described in the language of human imagination. Approaches to an unattainable goal are the only possibility. This, however, does not mean that man has no place or function at all in this universal conception. He belongs to this greater existence exactly in the same manner as each little star belongs to the total cosmos. However, he possesses power only in his small reality, and it is only this reality that he can recognize and control through his reason. The orders that reason has created in natural and in human objects are instruments of his human power. Like moral law and political systems, causal law and the periodic systems of elements have validity only as they are applied by and for men and are otherwise dead letters. In the religious conception of the world, and only here, this anthropocentric character is completely abandoned.

Our relationship to the general existence is, therefore, independent of the laws of reason and the symbols that man created (even though man believed he "discovered" them). Every personal life, too, is (to use a phrase of Lao-tse) integrated in "the all-powerful all-activity." The Hindus speak of the participation in the Sanskara: the endless renewal of existence, which is by no means only human or earthly. An explanation or description of such transcendency could be given only by the transcendency itself. Metaphysics, therefore, is the cause of its own destruction and can never succeed in replacing religion. From this stems the unfruitfulness of the Gnostics, of the religion of reason in the Age of Enlightenment, and of the different rationalistic proofs of God; for they all try to understand the "other world" with the means of our human world. The transcendental world confronts earthly reality as "the other one" and is necessary to our experience, necessary to our soul since it suffers from the inadequacy of our small reality. In the religious conception of life there is expressed not only the belief in the existence of "the other" but also the conviction that our human life is fatefully bound up with "the other"—in other words, the belief that we are part of a cosmic existence that is mysterious and wholly independent of our will. St. Augustine expressed this duality of the religious experience clearly and simply: "How did I burn with impatience, my God, to leave the earthly world and to flee back to Thee, and I did not know what Thou intend with me."

II

It is not necessarily a condition of the essential nature of religiosity that a specific object of religious belief must arise out of our emotion. To have a religious attitude to life it is sufficient that we believe in the general transcendency, in "the other" as the greater and mightier force of existence and destiny. Especially in religious life everything depends on movement, searching, and questioning, and nothing on the goal, the answer, or the object. Indeed, "the other," which is totally beyond all human categories, must by its very nature be beyond our imagination. Thus it has been said that God is simply the object of faith per se and that we can therefore say nothing more about Him. This means that belief in transcendency derives its creative strength from itself and sees in the deity only the supernatural place of all its objects. Faith produces its own object as a mere symbol of transcendency to which the ego attaches itself. All definitions of religiosity and religion agree that the object of religious belief lies beyond the sphere of human reality, even though religious experience itself is part of our human nature.

Whether religion is defined as the experience of the holy or the unconditional or—in the purely spiritualistic sense of Hegel and Schelling—as the realization of the absolute or objective spirit, the object of belief always lies beyond our earthly reality. If, in spite of that, no religion can exist without the concept of a personal God, the reason is the human need to consider the super-reality as a reality, too. The idea of a personal God is a metaphysical analogy to human life. Such a God embodies and symbolizes what is by His nature pure spiritual form.

But only by such symbolization (which includes myth, too) does religious feeling affect our lives and our attitudes in a way that could never be accomplished by a purely abstract conception of the Supreme Being or a refusal to imagine "the other" graphically. We give the general object of our belief a personal form, which signifies, at the same time, the highest perfection of our subjective being. Out of the consciousness of its own deficiency our ego produces the object of its belief as the *"ens perfectissimum."* And out of the suffering from all the contradictions in our human reality God arises as the *"coincidentia oppositorum,"* as the highest being, one in which all conflicts are eliminated.

In no religion is the idea of God as the highest symbol of "the other" represented in such purity as in Jewish monotheism. In contrast to the polytheistic religions, which in the multiplicity of their Gods try only to imitate the multifarious human world and thus remain limited to its ideas and experiences, Judaism abstracts the idea of one God as pure spirit. Certainly, preprophetic Israel still gave God Yahweh many human characteristics, but from the time of the Prophets these increasingly receded. This radical monotheism was taken over by Christianity, which, however, sought to temper the supernatural character of God through the mediating figure of Jesus, who through his human existence had to form a bridge from this world to the transcendental world.

The biblical command not to create an image of God clearly

demonstrates the tendency of the Jewish religion to remove the idea of the Supreme Being from the range of human imagination. The Bible emphasizes the impossibility of reproducing the form of God and thereby indicates the further impossibility of imagining God within the categories of our own reasoning and of comparing him with other phenomena. This incomparableness of God is especially emphasized by Isaiah: "To whom then will ye liken God? or what likeness will ye compare unto him?" (Isaiah 40:18). He lets God himself speak: "To whom then will ye liken me, or shall I be equal? saith the Holy One" (40:25). In Christianity, too, the purely spiritual character of God and the basic incapability of man to see God are emphasized. "God is spirit and they that worship Him must worship Him in spirit and in truth" (John 4:24). "Who only hath immortality, dwelling in the light which no man can approach unto; whom no man hath seen, nor can see . . ." (Timothy 6:16).

Thus, in religious experience God is the highest level of "the other": pure transcendency, universal fate, and omnipotence, to which all earthly beings are subject. If I turn to God, I want to free myself from earthly ties and to belong only to the highest and therefore incomprehensible world order on which alone I wish to be dependent. Every religious experience is a form of remembrance of this original transcendency as the highest cause, which is not conditioned by other causes or dependencies. "However, that which lies beyond life is the cause of life" (Plotinus).

The approach to God is completely different from the approach to human beings. Its object is distant and strange; it is a mysterious force that *we* cannot understand but that can and must understand *us* because we belong to its sphere of existence. It is the remembrance of the part of the original whole, or, in the sense of Lao-tse, the remembrance of the ego of the Tao, the unending pathway that moves eternally through space and time. This approach occurs in the form of an invocation of the Supreme Being. It is the call from a lower to a higher, from a smaller to a larger world. This relationship between subject and object is expressed in the very word *God*, since it has the same meaning in all Indo-European languages: He to whom I call. The Arabs begin their prayer with the "Labbaik" call:

"I am calling You to help me, O Allah, I call You, I call You." In the Bible, too, God is called as the highest authority of existence: "In my distress I cried unto the Lord and He heard me" (Psalm 120:1). "Lord, in trouble they have visited Thee, they poured out a prayer when Thy chastening was upon them" (Isaiah 26:16).

The call is no factual communication of man to God but, rather, the termination of an inner process in the ego. In its gradual conquering of earthly ties, the ego has approached the transcendency more and more and now wishes to be incorporated in it. Figuratively speaking: After having traveled such a great distance from its real and personal home up to the unfathomable transcendency of "the other," the soul now stands at the gate of the divine world and begs for admission. The fact that the prayers which follow the invocation also present certain wishes and ask for certain aid is of lesser importance for our consideration. It is, therefore, a rationalistic misunderstanding of prayer (to which even Kant succumbed) to think primarily and particularly of the demands it contains. In the call, in fervently turning toward "the other," the passions, the feelings, and volitional impulses of the soul are tied to the transcendental existence. The form is a call of religious ecstasy, a turning of the ego from empirical ties to a union with a higher world.

III

Religion is not metaphysics but a belief, at the center of which stands God, not man. Metaphysics, on the contrary, tries to understand existence by means of the categories of pure reason, which are inseparable from man.

Religion is a peculiar function of the soul to devote itself to a higher object which it produces. From this object emanates the meaning given to all existence, including human life. That is the meaning of the statement that God created man in his image.

Religion is not ethics. Ethics explains only the existence of moral law and examines the manifestations of good in individual and social life. Religion is the realm above ethics, the creative force from which the idea of goodness derives. While ethics has to do with regulating principles, religion proclaims the idea of morality as one of God's commandments, that is, as an essential element in our existence. God is, as Leibniz says, the postulate of moral belief. Thus in religion there is no discussion of the whys and wherefores of being good; moral action is self-evident because it is the consequence of man's religious nature. Since we try to overcome the small reality in which we live, we also rise above the injustice, the sins, and the evil actions that are part of this small reality. Only the recognition of moral insufficiency as a consequence of our this-worldly existence permits us to grasp the idea of pure goodness, which we must approach more and more. Good and evil, morality and sin thus are part of human nature; they are its attributes, which we must purify.

God has no attributes.

At least, the attributes that we ascribe to the Supreme Being are none in the sense of a human nature. To our way of thinking they are inconceivable. Only by endowing God with transcendental attributes (in the spirit of scholasticism) that are completely unknown to the human world, do we place him on the highest level of transcendency.

These attributes are as mysterious as the being whom we call God. We call God *holy*, and holy is the realm that he governs. In no way is holiness the same as goodness; it is not an ethical virtue. God's holiness signifies, rather, the perfection of His own existence, in contrast to the ever-imperfect, ever-defective human nature. God's holiness is the secret of secrets—namely, the secret of His existence. "Thy way, O God, is in the sanctuary" (Psalm 77:14), and therefore it is separated from all human ways. Man can never be holy, even if he is in full command of all ethical virtues. If nevertheless the Catholic Church canonizes its heroes of the faith, this distinction can have only approximate significance: because of their conduct, these people are closer to God's holiness than others.

The recognition of God's holiness is really the same as the belief in God: "And one cried unto another and said, Holy, holy, holy is the Lord of Hosts . . ." (Isaiah 6:3).

Eternity, too, is an attribute of God that lies beyond all human imagination. For us every existence has a beginning and an end. It is measurable. That is why eternity is the abolition of all forms of existence that we are able to perceive. Through God's eternity, through the everlasting creative process that He embodies, the holy "other" is moved into even deeper mystery, and the object of our belief becomes still more different in nature from our own believing, mortal, unholy selves. For man there are no approaches to the ideal of the eternal. Only God is eternal, only of him is it said: "Thy kingdom is an everlasting kingdom, and thy dominion endureth through all generations" (Psalm 145:13).

IV

We cannot know the holy and eternal God; Knowledge is possible only in the realm of empirical reality. Our soul's yearning for belief, however, makes this impossibility at the same time a necessity: as knowers we could not be believers; science would then be our only perception of the world and would exclude faith. Even art is bound to empirical reality, because artists must make use of matter in giving shape to their visions. Thus even the highest religious art can render religious experiences but cannot say anything about God.

Thus, in religion the relation between subject and object is completely different from what it is in science and art. Science tries to recognize reality by describing the lawful connections of its parts. Art transmutes an artist's creative emotion into subjective experiences and presents these in objective materials so that others, too, can understand the artistic works. In religion, however, we believe; we do not know; we do not give form. We believe as individuals, even though we may belong to a religious community and obey its precepts. We love God, each man according to his own belief.

In the religious view of the world, love of God has a meaning corresponding to knowledge in the scientific and form in the artistic world view. Through love of God the religious subject experiences its object and the total cosmic system of which God is the center. But since the object of this love belongs to transcendency, the way in which we experience it must be different from every earthly way of experiencing. Only in religious experience does the entire emotional strength of our soul stream forth unimpeded, since there no longer is any dependence on material reality.

We could call this love of God a religious perception if at the same time we emphasize the paradox inherent in this expression. It is, after all, a matter of a perception in which the object to be perceived arises from the feeling of the perceiving subject. We can say that the same function of our soul that originated the idea of God also recognizes Him. That is why we call it by this name: love.

The love of God has often been compared with earthly love. There, too, the lover creates his object, since, in his experience, he always changes and remodels the form of his loved one so that his own need for love is fulfilled. "In love, a new being arises which is attached to a certain personality, but which lives, in its nature and its idea, in a completely different world . . . " (Georg Simmel). In earthly love, too, the object appears after the subjective emotion that wishes to attach itself to somebody. Similarly, in erotic and in religious life, love has a moral strength that reacts on the lover: the object of his love is experienced as an ideal value that affects the lover with its ethical power. At the height of his passion for Frau von Stein, Goethe wrote words that could also be an expression of love for God: "I beg you on bended knees: complete your work, make me good!" She must be able to accomplish this, because, as his ideal, she also embodies the greatest goodness.

In Judaism and in Christianity, love of God as the true substance of religious experience is stressed again and again. We are to love God with all our heart, soul, and mind—that is, we must unite our entire self with him. For those who love God all things shall turn out for the best—that is, they will attain their human perfection. We can recognize the mutual nature of the love between God and man also in the idea of the covenant that God makes with the people of Israel.

That this kind of religious knowledge is mutual, that God, too, knows man in his love, is especially emphasized in Christianity: "But if any man loves God, the same is known of him" (1 Corinthians 8:3).

In the post-Biblical epochs and from various viewpoints, love of God is taught as true religious knowledge. Mysticism and rationalism, Meister Eckhart and Spinoza, agree on this point. The axiom of Christian mysticism is: "In tantum cognoscitur Deus, in quantum amatur" (God is recognized insofar as He is loved—St. Bernard). Love to Meister Eckhart is the "sweet union" that binds us to God and God to us. "He who has found this road need not search for another." Spinoza expresses the same thought when he sees salvation, blessedness, and freedom of man "in constant and eternal love of God or in God's love of man." He calls the recognition of the eternity of God "the spiritual love of God."

In the love of God the happy and thankful expectation is expressed that the bond with transcendency will enhance our own vital energies. As the insights of science increase our power over empirical reality, so does religious insight in the form of love of God increase our feeling for the greatness of existence. Any nihilism that may arise from the demolition of purely empirically bound values can be overcome by the conviction that far higher powers are at work and that we can choose to attach ourselves to them. Such a bond decreases temporal afflictions and sorrows. It is even capable of transforming the picture of the future, because it ties its ideals to goals that are above all temporality.

Amor Dei
An Approach to Spinoza's Philosophy of Religion

> He who loves God cannot strive that God should love him in return.
> —Spinoza, *Ethics*, 5, prop. 19.

I

Pantheism, or the identification of God with Nature, has been developed out of conflicting motives and in very different ways, according to the philosophies that originated it.

Thinkers of distinctive religious attitudes wanted to harmonize their beliefs with the scientific achievements of their times, while others were eager to replace traditional religious doctrines with the results of their own independent thinking. Often Pantheism is mystical in the East and intellectual in the West, animated by the idea of a unified world-picture. All pantheistic philosophies, however, reject the idea of a transcendent God outside the world and completely separated from it. God, they assert, has to be considered immanent to the world, to our mind as well as to all things.

Spinoza's proposition, "God is the indwelling and not the transitive cause of all things" (*Ethics*, 1, prop. 18), has often been condemned as atheism and materialism. Such an interpretation bewildered him to the utmost. In his letter to Jacob Ostens of February 1671 he wrote about one of his calumniators: "Does that man, I pray, cast aside all religion who declares that God must be recognized as the Highest Good, and that He must be loved as much with a free spirit?"[1] Regarding the reproach of atheism he added that such a defamation did no harm to him but only to the aggressor himself. He also emphasized that his concept of Nature has a purely spiritual character and that those who think "that God and Nature (by which they mean a certain mass, or corporeal matter) are one and the same, are entirely mistaken" (Letter to Henry Oldenburg, November or December, 1675).

It is obvious that Spinoza's strict monotheism is in harmony with his Jewish heritage. He did not hesitate, therefore, to assert (in the same letter): "And I would dare to say that I also agree with all the ancient Hebrews as far as it is possible to surmise from their traditions, even if they have become corrupt in many ways." But he added that he could not accept the Christian doctrine that God assumed human nature: "They (certain churches) seem to me to speak no less absurdly than if someone were to tell me that a circle assumed the nature of a square."

Such a religious philosophy makes the attempt to replace the mythological language of the Orient and of prehistorical days with Western conceptual thinking. In the Baroque period the view prevailed that God should not be believed in unless He is conceived by reason. Herbert of Cherbury established his "natural religion" on the basis of the intellect alike in all human beings.

Descartes offered several rational proofs for the existence of God. And even Pascal proclaimed that all human dignity is to be found in our thinking, but that we overcome the "prison" of the world by enjoining upon us the Infinite God.

Fundamentally all these philosophers are deeply religious, mostly clinging to the faith of their ancestors, even if they are critical toward the theological dogmas. Spinoza also has to be regarded as a representative of this crucial age. He agreed that his conceptual language is very different from that of the Scripture[2], but not his belief in God as a Being supremely perfect and absolutely infinite.

"He necessarily exists, He is one: He is, and acts solely by the necessity of His own nature; He is free cause of all things; all things are in God, and so depend on Him, that without Him they could neither exist nor be conceived; lastly, all things are predetermined by God, not through His free will or absolute fiat, but from the very nature of infinite power" (*Theologico-Political Treatise*, 6).

This train of thought is in distinctive contrast to the traditional dualism between God and World, Creator and Creation. In 1786, Moses Mendelssohn, who, in general, was a strong opponent of Spinoza's philosophy, stated in his essay *Moses Mendelssohn an die Freunde Lessings* that a "purified Spinozism" ("geläuterter Spinozismus") gets on well with Religion and Ethics and is especially compatible with Judaism. "Obviously the doctrine of Spinoza is much closer to Judaism than the orthodox doctrine of the Christians."[3] In the age of Romanticism Schelling developed his principle of the Absolute as presented in Nature as well as in Spirit, and, like Spinoza, used the word *God* as name for the Absolute, the synthesis of all contrasting principles.

Spinoza's early statement, "God is Truth" (*Short Treatise*, 2:15) goes far beyond the later proposition that God is Nature. We have to use all our intellectual tools in order to understand God as the "ultima veritas,"[4] and often our mind has to turn inward. Spinoza never became a fanatical rationalist, nor did he suppress the emotional forces in his soul.

It was on behalf of this emotional religiosity that, in 1877, Ernest Renan proclaimed in front of the Spinoza House in The Hague: "C'est d'ici peut-être que Dieu a été vu de plus près." ("It is from here perhaps that God was seen closest.")

II

It is characteristic for the fundamental difference between Eastern and Western philosophy that the idea of Love originated in the East as an ethical-metaphysical value, but in the West as a psychological experience.

Not only the Bible but Buddha's Speeches as well as the Koran and other Scriptures of oriental wisdom consider Love as a fountain of knowledge. According to Buddha all life strives to a loving union with the Brahma, the supreme being, towering far above all human desires. The biblical command Thou shalt love thy neighbor, the supreme law of Jewish-Christian Ethics, is overshadowed by the metaphysical-ethical command of the Love of God (or, in the words of Isaiah, that man has to be "servant of God"): "Thou shalt love the Lord with all thine heart, and with all thy soul, and with all thy might" (Deuteronomy 5:6). By loving God man serves the highest goal of his life and overcomes his mundane existence. It is this metaphysical idea of Love that Dante glorified at the end of the *Paradiso*: "L'Amor che move il sole e l'altre stelle" ("The love which moves the sun and the other stars" [*Paradiso*, canto xxxiii, v. 145]).

In contrast with this religious idea of Love of God is the Platonic doctrine of Eros, expounded especially in *Symposium* and *Phaedrus*, as an affective approach to the beauty of the sensual world.[5] Aristotle speaks about love only as a desire for existing things. In Western philosophy it is not before Neoplatonism that the idea of Love assumes the character of wisdom leading to a supreme good.

It is obvious that Spinoza's idea of Amor Dei follows the tradition of the Scripture and of Jewish postbiblical Literature of Wisdom. It is the link between his ethics and his ontology. In this idea we find pleasure which, in Spinoza's opinion, is the transition of a man from a lesser to a greater perfection. According to His very nature as the Being supremely perfect, God Himself is not affected by any emotion of pleasure or pain and does not love or hate. This kind of gladness or pleasure is also praised in Psalm 34: "My meditation of Him shall be sweet: I will be glad in the Lord."

In order to comprehend the religious motivation of Spinoza's idea of Amor Dei we have only to compare his attitude with that of Kant and his contempt of any kind of religious fanaticism or religious reverie (Religionsschwärmerei). For Kant Love of God is a nonrational affection, since God is no object for our senses, and furthermore, we cannot love by command, following the imperative "Thou shalt!"[6]

Such an argument would be without any validity for Spinoza since his concept of Love has nothing in common with sensuous affection. According to him the essence of Love is the desire of the lover to unite himself with the beloved object, "when it is absent, or of continuing in its presence when it is at hand" (*Ethics*, 3).[7] Already in his early writings Spinoza considered love as the only satisfying approach to God, to the Absolute. Also Saint Augustine had contrasted the Love of God, which he called "pure love" (caritas), with profane love, which to him seemed only covetousness. The Love of God, however, does not ask for any reward, for God Himself is the reward (*Enarrotiones in Psalms*, 134, 10). Time and again, Love of God had been revealed and interpreted as a chief motif in the Old and the New Testaments.

According to Spinoza only the love toward God makes us free from pain and satisfies our thirst for wisdom. Perishable objects produce in us fear, envy, or hatred. "But the love toward a thing eternal and infinite alone feeds the mind with pleasure, and it is free from all pain" (The Improvement of the Understanding, Introduction).

We are in the favorable position to be able to follow the history of Spinoza's idea of Amor Dei through his works and his correspondence. In the beginning, the impact of Judaism and late medieval mysticism prevails. In later years, his reflections take on a more intellectualistic character. In general we may say that his whole philosophical development is mirrored in his interpretation of this one motif.

III

In his interpretation of Amor Dei Spinoza tried to avoid two extremes: the extermination of religious feeling and the sacrifice of logical thinking. His attitude reminds us of Anselm of Canterbury: Credo ut intelligam, I believe so that I may understand.

Belief, that is to say, belongs to understanding, and it is not at all in contradiction to it. The "docta ignorentia," learned ignorance, has often been considered the highest stage of knowledge. Already in his first essay, *The Short Treatise* (Korte Verhandeling), Spinoza is a skeptic with regard to theological dogmas but by no means hostile to religion in general. Among the religious philosophers of the past it was especially Chasdai Crescas whom he deeply admired. In his letter to Lodovicus Meyer of April 1663 he spoke with great respect of him as "Rab Chasdai" and of his argument for the Unconditioned, the Absolute.

In the same treatise he called God the first cause, the cause of all things as well as the cause of Himself, the only substance in the world existing by itself. We can know Him alone through our love: "Love, then, arises from the idea and knowledge that we have of a thing; and accordingly as the thing shows itself greater and more glorious, so also is our love greater." And in the direction of the doctrine of unio mystica, the mystical union, he added: "Love is a union with the object which our understanding judges to be good and glorious." People who love transient things like pleasure, riches, and honor, love objects which have no reality whatever.[8] The union with God who presents perfection precedes the knowledge of things that follow the first cause. Love results from the understanding that the object of our knowledge is glorious and good. And Spinoza added in the manner of the Jewish Prophets: "What else, then, can follow but that it can be lavished upon no one more ardently than upon the Lord our God? For He alone is glorious, and a perfect good." True faith in God, therefore, means true knowledge, too, and true knowledge is attainable only through Love of God. In his letter to Henry Oldenburg of April 1662 Spinoza referred to the Short Treatise very modestly as his "opusculum." He repeated in this letter his concept of God as being identical with Nature and anticipated the persecutions by the theologians: "I am naturally afraid lest the theologians of our time take offence and with their usual hatred attack me who utterly loathe quarrels. . . . Things which they, on account of their prejudices, regard as created, I contend to be attributes of God, and as misunderstood by them; and also that I could not separate God from Nature as all of whom I have any knowledge have done."

Since God is unchangeable and steady, the love of Him is redemption from all evil, from all destroying passions in us. The union with God creates rest and peace of mind. It is this aspect of Spinoza's Amor Dei that Goethe glorified in *Faust* (Part I, Studierzimmer):

> Entschlafen sind nun wilde Triebe,
> Mit jedem ungestümen Tun;
> Es reget sich die Menschenliebe,
> Die Liebe Gottes regt sich nun.
>
> (The wild desires no longer win us,
> The deeds of passion cease to chain;
> The love of Man revives within us,
> The love of God revives again.)

It would be an arrant anthropomorphism to ask whether God loves man in return. Love and hatred belong to man and not to God, who is the indwelling in everything, its very essence, and neither a transient cause nor passionate like man. We have to pay homage to the world of God and not to superstition or the poetical images of antiquity.

From the *Short Treatise* on, the concept of Amor Dei remains the pivotal motif of Spinoza's philosophy. To be sure, it changed gradually from a mystical to an intellectual way of interpretation. But the philosopher always stressed the importance of the Love of God as means of deeper understanding, as a way of thinking, which has its own language, beyond, and further reaching than, our common tongue. God Himself does not need a language in order to communicate with human beings. In order to make Himself known to men, He needs neither words nor miracles, nor any other communication, but only Himself.

Spinoza went so far as to take the side of the pious people against the atheists. In his letter to Willem van Blyenbergh of January 5, 1663, he said that "the ungodly lack the love of God which springs from the knowledge of Him, and whereby alone we, according to our human understanding, are said to be the servants of God. Indeed, since they know not God, they are no more than a tool in the hand of the master which serves unconsciously and perishes in the service; on the other hand, the pious serve consciously and become more perfect by their service." And a few years later (letter to Ostens, February 1671), he called the love of God a "supreme injunction." "Whether I love God freely, or from the necessity of the decree of God, nevertheless I shall love God, and I shall be saved."

In spite of his excommunication by the Portuguese Synagogue in Amsterdam, Spinoza's adherence to the faith of his ancestors is revealed in his treatises as well as in his correspondence. But he attacked those people, Jews and Christians alike, who falsify religion by superstition or even by imposture. Never does the Scripture dispute reason if we would only interpret it in the right way.

The *Short Treatise* is followed and supplemented by the fragment *On the Improvement of the Understanding*. Time and again, Spinoza contrasted the Love of God and the more sensual love for transient things. The love for an object infinite and eternal nourishes our soul and is free from all disinclination. It is the love for the highest good and, therefore, the understanding of the unity of God and Nature.

At the time he wrote this fragment and also his treatise *Principles of Descartes' Philosophy Geometrically Demonstrated* Spinoza was already deeply involved in the completion of his main work, the *Ethics*. The essay on Descartes repeated and clarified his religious philosophy, especially his concept of God.

The *Theologico-Political Treatise* is Spinoza's first attempt to sum up his philosophical as well as personal development. Once again the reader witnesses the dramatic struggle of a thinker to overcome all narrow-minded bondages in order to reach a deeper and freer insight into the nature of God and Man. This Treatise (written probably between 1665 and 1670) became the beginning of a new field of study, biblical criticism, and of a philosophical interpretation of the Scripture. To be sure, it was written for an intellectual élite mature enough for such an interpretation. The deeply emotional preface is a personal credo combating bigotry and prejudices.

His philosophy never entirely moved away from religion, but his original mysticism changed more and more into rationalism. In a letter to Oldenburg (written in 1665), Spinoza spoke frankly about the reasons that led him to write this Treatise. "I am now writing a Treatise about my interpretation of Scripture. This I am driven to do by the following reasons: 1. the Prejudices of the Theologians; for I know that they are among the chief obstacles which prevent men from directing their mind to philosophy; and therefore I do all I can to expose them, and to remove them from the minds of the more prudent. 2. The opinion which the common people have of me, who do not cease to accuse me falsely of atheism; I am also obliged to avert this accusation as far as it is possible to do so. 3. The freedom of philosophizing, and of saying what we think; this I desire to vindicate in every way, for here it is always suppressed through the excessive authority and impudence of the preachers."

This freedom of philosophizing did not turn him away from his Love of God, but renewed it in a more philosophical, more abstract sense than before. The highest happiness of man, he repeats, is the understanding of the sublime Being, of God, through Love. We call *divine law* our realization of God's existence in our mind, and our doings are to be the consequence of the recognition of this law.

Fear of God, as many religions teach, and the expectation of punishment, are a great misunderstanding of the Love of God, which is man's greatest happiness and ultimate aim. The Treatise arrives, therefore, at the following conclusion:

"The idea of God lays down the rule that God is our highest good—in other words, that the knowledge and love of God is the ultimate aim to which all our actions should be directed. The worldling cannot understand these things, they appear foolishness to him, because he has too meager a knowledge of God, and also because in this highest good he can discover nothing which he can handle or eat, or which affects the fleshly appetites wherein he chiefly delights, for it consists solely in thought and the pure reason" (*Theologico-Political Treatise*, chap. 4).

Everyone, therefore, who is able to think and who knows that there is no greater gift than reason, must accept the divine law and the love of God as our greatest happiness and blessedness. Spinoza's treatment of the Love of God has, thus, to be considered as the first attempt to overcome the naive mythological or anthropomorphical interpretation of God, as the first step toward de-mythologizing religion and breaking with a tradition that believes in miracles instead of in reason and judgment. It was never in Spinoza's mind to replace faith by philosophy; instead he wanted to separate them and interpret the Scripture also from a rational standpoint. "Philosophy has no end in view save truth; faith, as we have abundantly proved, looks for nothing but obedience and piety" (*Theologico-Political Treatise*, chap. 14).

IV

Spinoza's Ethics, this gigantic intellectual edifice, completes his religious philosophy or philosophical religion. It would be a misinterpretation to call Spinoza a free-thinker or a Deist, like Toland, Shaftesbury, Tindal. He did not teach a "natural theology" in opposition to the traditional "revealed theology." In fact, Spinoza maintained that theology represented God as a "perfect man." "But in Philosophy, where we clearly understand that to apply to God the attributes which make a man perfect, is as bad as to want to apply to a man those which make perfect an elephant or an ass" . . . (Letter to Blyenbergh, March 13, 1665).

It is characteristic of Spinoza's general religious attitude that his *Ethics* begins with his *Doctrine of God*. The old Jewish tendency toward unification, toward oneness is prevailing. Behind the Baroque forms of the geometrical method and the formalistic construction of a logistic system a profound, penetrating, and sincere religiosity is always noticeable.

More even than the Treatises, the *Ethics* is detached from the mythological or poetical style of the Scripture. This is true also of Spinoza's presentation of the idea of Love of God. Instead of using the ancient formula of Amor Dei, he now coined the new phrase Amor Dei Intellectualis in order to convey the conviction that this kind of Love does not belong to the realm of emotions but is an instrument of our understanding. It is an understanding that leads us far beyond individual things. For God is the indwelling of all things, and all things are in Him.

God *is*: we know this by *intuition*, and we can prove it by deductions. For Spinoza the *scientia intuitiva*[9] is the third and highest kind of knowledge, following perceptual experiences and conceptual understanding. "From this kind of knowledge arises pleasure accompanied by the idea of God as cause, that is the Love of God; not insofar as we imagine Him as present, but insofar as we understand Him to be eternal; that is what I call the intellectual love of God" (*Ethics* 5).

This is the ultimate, the classical definition of Spinoza's idea of Amor Dei. The Christian concept is quite different. It is true that St. John (First Epistle General, 4:16) said similarly to Spinoza: "God is love, and he that dwelleth in Love dwelleth in God." However, he also said: "We love Him, because He first loved us." Such a love as appreciation of the blessings that God has bestowed on us would, according to Spinoza, have no metaphysical meaning.

The love of God toward men is identical with His love of Himself. "The intellectual love of the mind toward God is that very love whereby God loves Himself, not insofar as He is infinite, but insofar as He can be explained through the essence of the human mind regarded under the form of eternity, in other words, the intellectual love of the mind toward God is part of the infinite love wherewith God loves Himself."

Hence it follows for Spinoza that, in contrast to the doctrine of St. John, the intellectual love of the mind toward God and the love of God toward men have to be considered as identical. Our constant, eternal love toward God is our freedom, our blessedness, our salvation. In this connection Spinoza refers to the Bible, which calls this love or blessedness also glory, and not undeservedly. It may also be called acquiescence of spirit, which is not really distinguished from glory.[10] "In proportion as the mind understands more things by the universal and intuitive kinds of knowledge, it is less subject to those emotions, which are evil, and stands in less fear of death." God Himself is free of all passions and never affected by joy or by sadness, by pleasure or by pain. Again in contrast to St. John, Spinoza asserts that God does not love or hate. It is the climaxing statement of Spinoza's religious philosophy that man cannot expect a reward for his love of God. "He who loves God cannot strive that God should love him in return." Such an expectation would abolish the true idea of God since we know that He acts solely through the laws of His own nature and is without passions. In very plain language the same train of thought was expressed in Spinoza's letter to Jacob Ostens of February 1671: that we have to love God as the highest good, "not from fear of some punishment (for love cannot spring from fear) nor for love of some other object, by which we hope to be gratified, for then we should not so much love God Himself as that which we desire." From the assumption that God is a substance of infinite attributes it follows that the love of God provides us with the knowledge of good and evil, since nothing can be bad that is in harmony with our nature. Good is, therefore, that which satisfies our longing, and the highest object of our longing is God Himself.

Only through the abolishment of the distinction between the Creator and his creatures does the intellectual love toward God become identical with God's love toward Himself and toward the universe. "Hence it follows that God, insofar as He loves Himself, loves man and, consequently, that the love of God toward men, and the intellectual love of the mind toward God are identical." Such an identification changes the moral imperative: "Thou shalt love God" to a metaphysical maxim embracing every kind of existence. Even death loses its horror by the understanding of it through the love of God.

The more our mind understands, the less subject we are to evil emotions and to fear of death.

V

Spinoza's philosophical development from a mystical to a highly intellectual concept of the Love of God did not at all detract from the religious impetus of his thinking. It is often overlooked how close his viewpoint was to the Jewish philosophy of the Middle Ages. Chasdai Crescas, for instance, usually considered an irrationalist, called the Love of God the highest good and the final goal of our human existence. It follows from the very nature of love that the union with God is the result of the love of Him. Abraham Ibn Daud, before him, explained that both the understanding of God and the Love of God are the very aim of humanity, in which alone happiness and perfection can be found. Even Maimonides taught that the love of God is in proportion with our knowledge of Him. In the Renaissance Leone Ebreo (Abravanel) wrote his *Dialoghi d'Amore* in the direction of Neoplatonism, but also under the impact of Cresca's interpretation of the Bible.[11]

The idea of Love of God never ceased to occupy the thoughts of Spinoza. In one of his last letters to Henry Oldenburg (February 7, 1676) he wrote once again about "the true knowledge and love of God." "He who is unable to control his desires, and to restrain them through fear of the laws, although he must be excused for his weakness, is nevertheless unable to enjoy peace of mind, and the knowledge and love of God, but necessarily perishes."

The love of God is, therefore, the very clue to every understanding, to every knowledge. It took more than a century before the religious nucleus of this philosophy was revealed. Novalis, the poet, called Spinoza, the alleged atheist, "gotttrunken" (drunken with God), and it was the German theologian Friedrich Schleiermacher who expressed his admiration for the great pantheist in these enthusiastic words:

"Ihn durchdrang der hohe Weltgeist, das Unendliche war sein Anfang und sein Ende, das Universum seine einzige und ewige Liebe; in heiliger Unschuld und tiefer Demut spiegelte er sich in der ewigen Welt." (Über die Religion [Berlin 1799]). ("He was imbued with the high Spirit of the World, the Infinite was his beginning and his end, the universe his only and eternal love. In holy innocence and deep humility he mirrored himself in the eternal world.")

NOTES

1. All letters are quoted from the edition of *Spinoza's Correspondence* by A. Wolf, (London, 1928), his works from the translation by H. M. Elwes, (London, 1889).
2. He emphasized that the styles of the Old and of the New Testament are quite similar, in spite of the fact that the first was written in Hebrew, the second in Greek, but both were written by Hebrews (*Theological-Political Treatise*, 7).
3. Heinrich Scholz, ed., *Die Hauptschriften zum Pantheismusstreit zwischen Jacobi und Mendelssohn* (Berlin, 1915), p. 295.
4. Even the Portestant theologian Karl Barth affirmed: "The creed of Christian faith rests upon knowledge. . . . Faith means knowledge" (*Dogmatics in Outline* [New York, 1941]).
5. To be sure, sometimes (e.g. in *Lysis*) Plato asserts that love and friendship show the aspiration toward a final goal, but this goal is not presented as a metaphysical-ethical value.
6. *Critique of Practical Reason*, Pt. I, Bk. I, Chap. 3.
7. Therefore, we might love and fear God at the same time. In the Old Testament Jesus Ben Sirach, too, emphasized that Love and Fear of God do not exclude each other.
8. Especially this train of thought is close to the teachings of Buddhism. Cf. S. M. Melamed, *Spinoza and Buddha* (Chicago, 1933).
9. It is obvious that Bergson's concept of intuition is closely related to that of Spinoza. Bergson himself denied categorically that when speaking about intuition he meant instinct or feeling: "And in everything I have written there is assurance to the contrary: my intuition is reflection" (*The Creative Mind* [New York, 1946], p. 103.)
10. Spinoza refers to Isaiah 6:3: "And one cried unto another, and said, Holy, holy, holy, is the Lord of hosts: the whole earth is full of his glory."
11. The standard work by Harry Austryn Wolfson, *The Philosophy of Spinoza*, 2 vols. (Cambridge, Mass., 1934) elaborates on this relation between Spinoza and medieval Jewish philosophy in detail. About the Love of God cf. 2:276 ff.

Intuition and Knowledge
On the Henri Bergson Centennial, October 18, 1959

> Which among the philosophies will endure? I do not know. But I hope that philosophy itself will endure forever.
>
> —Schiller

I

To understand the incomparable effect of Henri Bergson's writings one must recall the intellectual situation of Europe at the turn of the century.

Philosophy had rigidified into a mechanistic methodology of abstract concepts. Any quest for the ultimate questions and answers, for the meaning of life and the highest values and principles of existence was rejected as "unscientific." The triumphs of the natural sciences induced philosophy to emulate their exact methods. Nietzsche, that prophetic genius, had warned against "the mechanistic clumsiness" of the natural sciences; but academic philosophy gradually abandoned what had, since the ancient Greeks, been hallowed ground and contented itself with the barren, formalistic soil. There were, to be sure, thinkers who sought to break out of the narrow confines of logical definitions and pointed to the limitations of the scientific method. But the universities turned a deaf ear to the ardent quest of the age, to its profound crisis of faith and its longing for new ideas. For spiritual help people had to turn to the poets and to prophetic spirits like Nietzsche, Tolstoy, and the religious sages of the East.

This was the situation when the first books of Henri Bergson appeared. They went far beyond the aim of a critique of contemporary philosophy and opened new and unexpected aspects to consideration.

From the outset these writings did not shun metaphysics but saw in it the real task of philosophy. The struggle of this thinker to oppose to conventional intellectualism the intuitive power of experience is something stirring. *Matière et Memoire* (1896) marks the beginning of Bergson's philosophy of intuition, of the *élan vital*. It extended to aesthetics (*Le Rire*, 1900) and to ethics and the philosophy of religion (*Les deux Sources de la Morale et de la Religion*, 1932). The little masterpiece *Introduction à la Metaphysique* (1903) and *L'Evolution Créatrice* (1907) are at the center of his work. Bergson's profound and enduring influence on contemporary French literature, particularly on Charles Péguy and Marcel Proust, is a measure of his linguistic style and the mode of his thought.

With passionate words Bergson deplores the sad impoverishment of the human psyche under the burden of technical and material progress. "Half crushed to death, mankind sighs under the burden of the progress it has made." Instead of a mechanistic view of the world he teaches a vitalistic one; instead of logical analysis he offers a visionary synthesis, putting the experience of the absolute in the place of conceptual symbols; in place of a description of objects from without he offers intuition, "the kind of intellectual empathy that enables one to put oneself inside an object in order to get at the unique and inexpressible elements it possesses." Thus philosophy becomes an intellectual and emotional participation, a painful effort we make to penetrate to the heart of objects.

Bergson's great erudition enabled him to adduce for his

philosophy of intuition examples from the fields of biology, psychology, physics, art, and religion. His skill in presentation is so great that one must rank him among the greatest masters of French prose. The intellect—so he assures us—can think only in material terms and is incapable of grasping the true nature of life. Thus science and metaphysics are two antithetical kinds of knowledge. Metaphysics must go beyond the world of concepts; it must reach intuition in order to comprehend through the self the world and the self.

II

The idea of intuition as an instrument of knowledge is not so novel as it may seem. Maimonides had already spoken of the limitation of our intellect which, so he said, was sufficient only for earthly reality. He pointed to the power of the intuitive insights of the biblical prophets. Spinoza, who was unjustly decried as a stubborn rationalist, declared in the manner of a mystic that the highest type of knowledge was union with God, the fountainhead of all truth and all being, and that this union was possible only through intuition.

Bergson presented intuition as the absolute antithesis of scientific knowledge. As the ancient Greeks had done, he brought it closer to art and religion. In fact, he proclaimed the self-abolition of reason as the real goal of philosophy, so that "through the imposition of a definite discipline our mind may become capable of leading us to a philosophy that will outgrow it."

The boldness of such an enterprise is as dangerous as it is astonishing. It is the expression of a passionate will to life. "No longer a conceptual eternity, which is an eternity of death, but an eternity of life!" That is why Bergson regards it as the foremost task of the world to bring forth gods. We are privileged to attach our existence to irrational beings.

With such statements the realm of reason is considerably curtailed and even undermined. Bergson's irrationalism was bound to fail when he attempted to attack the mechanistic foundations of physics as well. It is not possible to apply the biological concept of *élan vital*, the drive of life, to inanimate reality in time and space. The purely psychological passage of time inside us has nothing to do with the causal connection of events outside us.

The *durée*, Bergson's new conception of time, designates the unbroken flow of experience and is related to the Heraclitean idea of change. "Without the survival of the past in the present there would be no permanence, but only a momentary existence." It is thus a matter of historical processes in the realm of human life. That we remember the past and experience it as present by virtue of our memory is a characteristic quality of human nature. But is this ability to remember the same as objective time, the intuitional form of our thinking that we utilize in an attempt to recognize reality outside ourselves? Bergson properly says: "It is our self that endures." That is why our past is not lost to us; rather, it follows us as an indivisible evolution that cannot be represented conceptually. "The *durée* is the continuous life of a memory that continues the past in the present."

We know what a great influence Bergson's purely psychological doctrine of time has had on literature. It is the key to an understanding of Marcel Proust's novels. On physics and mathematics, however, it had no effect, because both sciences concern themselves with measurements and cannot do without definite concepts.

III

The intellectual revolution that is associated with the name of Henri Bergson began early and is far from being at an end today. It means the rebellion of the psyche against reason, of passion against mechanism and materialism. It brought about a new flowering of all metaphysical motives of thought and action. Like Nietzsche, James, and Whitehead, Bergson endeavored to bridge the gulf between philosophy and life.

This anti-intellectualism became especially important for religious life—not in the sense of a particular creed, but for the religious attitude in general. This attitude is determined by all disappointments that life causes us. "Religion," Bergson writes, "is that which should make up a possible deficit for beings gifted with reflection." A true experience of God is rare, but "when it is given voice, something appears deep down in most people that imperceptibly responds to it."

There seem to be frequent points of contact between Bergson's philosophy of religion and Catholicism. For his own person he categorically refused to convert. In his testament of 1937 he stated: "My reflections have brought me close to Catholicism. I see in it the fulfillment of Judaism. I might have become a convert, but for many years I have observed the terrible wave of anti-Semitism that has engulfed the world. I prefer to remain among those who will be the persecuted tomorrow."

His fame and his academic rise began early. In the year 1900 he was appointed to the chair in philosophy at the Collège de France, and in 1928 he received the Nobel Prize for Literature.

Henri Bergson's last years were the most painful of his life. A serious malady, which he tried to endure with patience, grew worse when France collapsed and was occupied by the Germans. The Nuremberg Laws were introduced in Paris as well. With his last strength the mortally ill man dragged himself to the prefecture to register as a Jew.

He died in 1941.

(translated by Harry Zohn)

Aspects of the Jewish Question

> For sufferance is the badge of all our tribe.
> —Shakespeare, *The Merchant of Venice*, I, III.

The story of Diaspora Jewry is rich in paradoxical situations. There is no greater paradox, however, than the fact that the European Emancipation at the beginning of the nineteenth century, which was intended to do justice to the Jews and to provide a happier life for them, made their situation more problematic and complicated than it had been before. All civil rights were bestowed on them and the doors to European civilization opened widely. In fact, they became active and creative in all Western cultural fields and yet they never became completely integrated into the surrounding nations. They were considered by many gentiles as noncomformists, clinging to their past, and as strangers in the Christian society. They retained their old spiritual nationality, the residuum of their ancestry, which they kept alive, sometimes even when they had lost their religious belief or had become converted to Christianity.

The Emancipation started in France. To be sure, the secret intention of those who advocated it was the abolition of all Jewish community life. Very characteristic is a speech made in 1789 by Clermont-Tonnere in the French National Assembly: "Everything should be refused to the Jews as a nation, but everything should be granted to them as individuals." According to him the Jews should renounce their organizations in order to discontinue the state of estrangement between themselves and the gentiles. Two years before, in 1787, the great liberal statesman Count Mirabeau published his stirring book, *About Moses Mendelssohn and the Political Reforms of the Jews*, in which he advocated the termination of all civic restrictions on the Jews and asked his fellow-citizens to help them attain the cultural level of the European nations, adding: "The Jew is above all a human being before being a Jew." But when, in 1791, civic rights were extended to the Jewish inhabitants of France, it became obvious soon afterwards that a complete symbiosis or amalgamation could not be accomplished.

There were, and still are, people who believe that Reform Judaism should not only narrow the gap between Christians and Jews, but also establish a Jewish religion independent of the national Jewish community life. For this reason early Reform Judaism was sometimes called another "Christian sect." It is significant to know that also in this form Judaism did not lead to any Jewish missionary activities among non-Jews. It remained an inner affair of the Jewish people, in spite of the attempts by the reformers to eliminate all allusions to the Jewish nation from prayerbooks and religious customs.

Again experience showed that people are able to change habits and institutions, but they are unable to change their past, their heritage, which shapes individuals as well as groups. We can educate our children according to a modern ideology, but we cannot destroy the impact of our ancestors, effective from one generation to the other. In this historic experience is to be found the reason for the phenomenon that the cultural and social assimilation of the Jews never reached its final goal, the complete integration into the surrounding nations. The Jews survived as a minority group, continuing the past and distinguished not only by a different religious faith but also by many cultural and psychological features. Because of this enigmatic power of survival, Nietzsche considered the Jews as "the strongest, the toughest and the purest race that is now living in Europe." The fight against them, therefore, had always been "a sign of the lower envious and cowardly nature, and he who now takes part in it must carry in him a great deal of vulgar sentiment."

In the course of the nineteenth century the religious issue lost its power in the relationship between the Jews and their surroundings. Especially in Protestant countries positivistic philosophy and its hostile attitude toward religion in general developed an indifference in all matters of faith. Thinkers like Feuerbach, Comte, Darwin, Haeckel either avoided the discussion of religious truth, or they denied emphatically its existence. The tension between Jews and gentiles, however, went on, demonstrating thereby that it was caused by factors other than the difference of religious teachings. Since the industrial revolution social sciences gradually replaced any kind of metaphysics and even ethics was traced back to the social facts of life. The Jews, too, were, and are, therefore, considered only a social group separated from other groups by inherited biological, intellectual, and psychological features.

In his novel *Doctor Zhivago*, the late Russian poet of Jewish descent, Boris Pasternak, asks the Jews why they never gave up fighting and being massacred. He gives the answer himself: because they have to follow the command of their spiritual heritage. On the other hand, no gentile would say to the Jews: "You are the first and best Christians in the world."

It is, therefore, this indefinable spiritual heritage that caused the survival of the Jews. They were the founders of two monotheistic religions and also in the front line of many ethical-social movements in modern history. This fact is the best argument against the assertion that they are a "fossil remnant of antiquity" (Toynbee). In the pursuit of their religious-ethical tradition they became the opponents of many political ideologies of the modern world: will to power, despotism, militarism, thirst for conquest, etc. Jewish history in the Diaspora presents the Jews as a peaceful people deeply devoted to their countries.

The sociologist P. A. Sorokin coined the term *biosocial group*. Such a group is characterized by a certain mixture of biological and sociocultural traits. The more it differs from the majority, the more it is hated and persecuted. The consequence is isolation and seclusion of the minority.

Surprisingly enough the whirl of modern life has not abolished the tension between the different biosocial groups. As the smallest minority, without any political ambition, the Jews became the scapegoats in the conflicts between the powerful competing social groups, like nations, classes, professions, and their ideologies.

In the modern heterogeneous or pluralistic society the Jews live mostly as city-dwellers. As such they have developed a more reflexive mind and are bound more to their houses than to nature. There is a certain legitimacy in calling them a "psychological race," especially as far as their sense of criticism and of self-criticism is concerned. It is an attitude similar to the one Socrates adopted in Plato's "Phaedrus" when Phaedrus stated that Socrates never ventured outside the gates of the city: "Very true, my good friend," answered Socrates, "and I hope that you will excuse me when you heard the reason, which is that I am a lover of knowledge, and the men who dwell in the city are my teachers, and not the trees or the country."

This exclusive life as city-dwellers and "lovers of knowledge" may be traced back, of course, to the medieval ghettos in which the Jews had been compelled to live in complete seclusion, separated from nature as well as from many professional activities. This fact explains many "Jewish traits" that cannot be traced back to the concept of a biological race.

To be sure, Jewish "otherness" is a coherent process and can be comprehended only through the unique Jewish history. Those who do not want to accept any kind of "otherness" or group individuality speak about the "social abnormality" of the Jews and eventually of other minority groups, too. They are hostile toward them as they are hostile to foreigners whose languages they cannot understand. They are self-assured, clinging to standardization of all men along their own lines.

This is the crucial issue of modern anti-Semitism and its distinctive nationalistic character. Since it is irrationalistic by nature, it cannot be refuted by logical arguments. The anti-Semitic ideologies of our time are, therefore, the primitive disguises of this hostility of majority groups against everything in the world that seems to be strange or heterogeneous or incomprehensible. The anti-Semitic outbursts in our age can be regarded as iconoclastic riots in the name of standardization or normalization of the uniform masses.

The psychology of this social anti-Semitism as a vulgar resentment of the majority against a minority group is especially revealed by Jean-Paul Sartre in his brilliant essay "Portrait of the Anti-Semite" (1946): "The Jew is only a pretext: elsewhere it will be the Negro, the yellow race; the Jew's existence simply allows the anti-Semite to nip his anxieties in the bud by persuading himself that his place has always been cut out in the world, that it was waiting for him and that by virtue of tradition he has the right to occupy it. Anti-Semitism, in a word, is fear of man's fate. The anti-Semite is the man who wants to be a pitiless stone, furious torrent, devastating lightning: in short, everything but a man."

It is obvious, therefore, that the so-called "Jewish question" is much more a question of the surroundings than of the Jews themselves. It must be discussed not only in regard to the Jews living in the Diaspora but in regard to modern society in general. Anti-Semitism is a social passion directed against the Jews as well as against other minority groups which do not seem to fit into the picture of a uniform society.

Facing the future we must say that the position of the Jews of the Diaspora will depend on the general social-psychological conditions of the world. In other words, since there is no isolated Jewish question, there also can be no isolated "solution."

In principle, we have to face two extreme possibilities:

1) Human society could become even more homogeneous and uniform. The nationalistic feelings of the masses as a kind of self-assurance would be even more hostile to minority groups and foreigners than today.

However, after a period of such uniformity or national egoism, people would feel the need for higher and universal values. Such a new universalism (which in the past revealed itself mostly in the form of a new religion or of a social revolution) would embrace also the minority groups, perhaps many nations and, therefore, demote the ideal of a homogeneous, uniform society. The mind would be directed to higher goals than the hostilities between men and men.

2) The age of social uniformity could be followed by the countermovement of a new individualism (as it happened at the end of the Middle Ages when the Renaissance movement started). The variety of social types or minority groups would consequently be considered as a general advantage for society and no longer as a misfortune. This would apply to the Jewish minority, too, and would guarantee its continued peaceful coexistence with the majority groups.

Herbert Spencer established the law of integration and differentiation as fundamental for life in general. If the present stage of integration in social history would be followed by a stage of differentiation, the ideal of social-biological normality would have to be sacrificed and the existence of the Jews in the Diaspora would no longer be called an abnormality. The diversity of the human race would be considered rather as its very nature.

We have to add that the Jews themselves are highly individualistic and present a unity only in the manifoldness of variation. Goethe compared them with the Germans in this respect and saw in this individualism the best guaranty for their survival: "The Germans will not perish, as little as the Jews, since they are individuals."

Only a totalitarian society feels the obligation to persecute the minority groups and to reject the idea of coexistence. When the idea of diversity is accepted for the human society, mutual understanding and mutual aid become the moral law for all social groups.

A new form of heterogeneousness, of individualistic differentiation would reestablish the common belief in the dignity of men as free beings and no longer as members of national, social, or religious groups only.

Jewish Thoughts

There is no more profound parable of Jewish fate than the legend of Jacob's dream. On his way from Beersheba to Haran, far from the safe human settlements and all alone, Jacob rests on hard desert ground. But in his dream he builds the ladder that leads from the rocky, painful earth to the opened heaven, and he is permitted to speak to God.

Hillel taught: "If I am not for myself, who will be? And if not now, when?" But it is always easier to help others than oneself, and it is always possible to cope with tomorrow better than with today.

It is the tragedy of the Jews of the Diaspora that they possess a great and long past and yet are not a people with a history. The past is the sum of all our variable experiences, the ups and downs of life in days and centuries. But history is the evolving reality of a people and a country, the national self that lives through these experiences. For a people with a history, the future is the continuation of a long road. But a people without history is always at the beginning. The historical reality of the Jewish people lies in the spiritual, in the religious, in the transcendence of God. Like Pascal, the Jews can pray: "My changes and transformations do not change Thee. Thou art always the same, though I am very changeable."

Jewish Messianism resembles Schopenhauer's metaphysics of the will; both put the goal of their efforts at a distance that can never be attained. But the Messianic faith is creative; it is oriented toward life and gives us the strength to endure suffering for the sake of the coming redemption. Schopenhauer's doctrine of the will negates life, since only lack of will, and thus nothingness, can bring salvation.

The Jews have always been the true "good Europeans." The great European tension between reason and emotion, reality and dream, West and East is in them, and it is the secret of their creativity. Spinoza was a rationalist and a mystic at the same time, and the Hasidic mystics were sophists and hairsplitters like the Talmudists.

The recognition that there is no definitive solution of the Jewish problem relieves us neither of the duty to try all solutions nor of the obligation to be Jews.

(translated by Harry Zohn)

A Note about the Editor and Translators

HARRY ZOHN, a close associate and friend of Rudolf Kayser in the last dozen years of the latter's life, is the Viennese-born Professor of German and Chairman of the Department of Germanic and Slavic Languages at Brandeis University. He has published widely on Jewish writers of German-speaking countries, and among his numerous translations are the complete Zionist writings of Theodor Herzl.

Israeli-born TALI PERLMAN did her translations of Kayser's fiction as a Brandeis freshman enrolled in Dr. Zohn's course "The Jewish Contribution to German Literature."